Literature-Based Social Studies: Children's Books & Activities to Enrich the K-5 Curriculum

By Mildred Knight Laughlin and Patricia Payne Kardaleff
Oryx Press 1991

The rare Arabian Oryx is believed to have inspired the myth of the unicorn. This desert antelope became virtually extinct in the early 1960s. At that time several groups of international conservationists arranged to have 9 animals sent to the Phoenix Zoo to be the nucleus of a captive breeding herd. Today the Oryx population is nearly 800, and over 400 have been returned to reserves in the Middle East.

Copyright © 1991 by The Oryx Press
4041 North Central at Indian School Road
Phoenix, Arizona 85012-3397

Published simultaneously in Canada

Printed and Bound in the United States of America

∞ The paper used in this publication meets the minimum requirements of American National Standard for Information Science—Permanence of Paper for Printed Library Materials, ANSI Z39.48, 1984.

Library of Congress Cataloging-in-Publication Data

Laughlin, Mildred.
    Literature-based social studies : children's books and activities to enrich the K–5 curriculum / by Mildred Knight Laughlin and Patricia Payne Kardaleff.
    p. cm.
Includes bibliographical references and index.
ISBN 0-89774-605-8
1. Social sciences—Study and teaching (Elementary) 2. Social sciences—Study and teaching (Elementary)—Bibliography.
3. Activity programs in education. 4. Teaching—Aids and devices.
I. Kardaleff, Patricia Payne. II. Title.
LB1584.L38 1991   90-46103
372.83—dc20   CIP

For Mildred's daughters
Barbara and Debra
and
Pat's husband
Steven

Contents

Introduction:
Using Children's Literature in
the Teaching of Social Studies

THEORETICAL BACKGROUND FOR CHOICE OF UNITS AND OBJECTIVES

Regardless of the approach to teaching elementary school social studies, the literature-based method will enrich the program. If social studies is taught without a textbook, appropriate children's literature is essential. If a textbook is used for basic information and concepts, it is necessary that children have access to other materials in order to encourage individual exploration and to provide problem-solving situations. George Maxim in *Social Studies and the Elementary School Child* stresses that children should have pleasant experiences with a variety of trade books in their social studies classes. He emphasizes the use of more than the biographies and information books usually associated with the social studies curriculum. He believes that adventure stories, realistic stories, and folktales are also valuable sources to stimulate curiosity and motivate further exploration on a topic of interest.[1]

In the development of this work the authors found an abundance of children's books to enrich a K-5 social studies curriculum. Because of the literary quality of the books and their significant content, it was not difficult to create enjoyable sharing activities. The problem the authors faced was to develop units of work that were common to many social studies programs. With the abandonment of social studies texts in many districts and the increased emphasis on multicultural education, the selection of appropriate units for the introduction of valuable children's literature books became a formidable task.

"What shall we select from our social heritage to form the solid core of citizenship training? What common understanding and behavior provide the cement which holds our society together?"[2] Decisions concerning these two questions, posed by Paul Hanna in *Assuring Quality for the Social Studies in Our Schools*, have been at the root of many changing approaches to the social studies curriculum in the twentieth century. Those who propose new approaches will agree with Hanna that it is not a simple matter to select and organize significant content from our historical and contemporary social heritage.

Perhaps the most common area of agreement by the creators of elementary social studies programs was identified by George Maxim in *Social Studies and the Elementary School Child.* He suggests, "Perhaps the most comprehensive objective of the social studies curriculum is helping young children become good citizens."[3] Although he admits that no two sources concur exactly on the types of pupil competencies essential for good citizenship, three general categories of agreement involve gaining knowledge and understandings, acquiring social studies skills, and developing attitudes and values.

In developing the units and objectives for this present work, the authors made use of the report of the Curriculum Task Force of the National Commission on Social Studies in the Schools. This document, entitled *Charting a Course: Social Studies for the 21st Century*, proposes a number of grade level and content goals that became a basis for this book's units and objectives.[4] It is assumed that the task force recommendations will be considered by many social studies curriculum committees in the next decade.

Basic to the task force's content goals for kindergarten through grade three was the need for opportunities to make appropriate classroom decisions so that children would acquire individual and group participation skills. By examining families at home and far away, children should gain insight into commonalities and differences and should develop the understandings needed to contribute to a changing world. As the study of families extends to communities, the children need to know about the community in which they live and the national traditions important to responsible citizens. Vital also is an understanding of pioneer communities, Native American communities, and groups of people in other parts of the world who live under differing environmental and social conditions. Geography skills need to be and are easily integrated into kindergarten through third grade units. Each new geographic area can be located on maps and globes so that by the completion of grade three children will have received a basic introduction to world geography.

As recommended by the task force, heroes should be introduced in K-3 through discussion of the contributions of a variety of Americans. The examination of folklore, holidays, and customs in various countries of the world should also be highlighted. American cultural diversity should not be neglected in the choice of books to include in this work.

United States history is the focus for grades four and five as identified in the task force report. Basic historical documents are introduced. Individuals and groups responsible for the development of the nation receive attention. The challenges faced by Native Americans also are included. Geography skills continue to receive emphasis.

In creating this work the authors were cognizant of the increased emphasis on multicultural education as trade books and activities were chosen. As Christine Bennett asserts in *Comprehensive Multicultural Education*, "The challenge to become knowledgeable about new ethnic and national perspectives may seem overwhelming at first, but it is a challenge that teachers are obliged to meet."[5] Two of her suggestions for possible ways of proceeding were particularly useful in preparing this work. She advised that it is appropriate to "start small." It is feasible to begin by selecting one or two nations or ethnic groups to share that have significant meaning to the children. Then one can become acquainted with community resources that will provide information about these selected nations or ethnic groups. A list of appropriate local residents can be compiled who would visit the school or allow students to interview them.

After determining the unit topics, objectives, and recommended readings, the authors attempted to develop a variety of activities to make sharing pleasurable and worthwhile. Resource persons, realia, field trips, maps, construction activities, art activities, creative dramatics, and creative writing were basic vehicles for learning that were utilized. It is hoped that users of this book will find the choice of objectives, content, and activities appropriate to their needs.

HOW THIS BOOK IS ORGANIZED AND HOW IT CAN BE USED

The units that follow are suggested ideas for extending the social studies curriculum beyond the adopted text or the scope and sequence developed in the local school district or at the state level. It was impossible to select units that would fit every curriculum at all times, but it was assumed that the design for social studies in many districts would, in general, begin with the family, extend to the community, and by grades four and five be concerned with the history of the United States from its beginning to the present.

This may be considered a traditional approach, but the recommendations of the task force identified earlier make it seem a legitimate one. Within this framework, the objectives, recommended readings, and activities evidence a constant recognition of the nation's cultural diversity and of the need for children to know and respect world neighbors.

The units developed for each grade level are organized in a similar pattern. Each individual unit identifies objectives to be accomplished by using the trade books suggested. The objectives are written to be behavioral outcomes for students that teachers may use when preparing lesson plans. Knowledge and comprehension skills are basic for the objectives. Higher cognitive levels of application, analysis, synthesis, and evaluation become more evident as progress through the grades is made. Each unit includes a bibliography of recommended readings, provides a teacher or school library media specialist with an introductory activity, and suggests follow-up activities for teachers and students to share.

For kindergarten, transition, and first grade, the teacher will read books aloud and will direct activities. The brief annotations for the recommended books are descriptive in nature, as the activity related to the book provides a more detailed use guide. The objectives to be achieved by the activity are indicated following each annotation.

In the second- and third-grade units, many of the suggested activities are more self-directed. Children may be asked to do research in the library media center, interview an adult, write a paragraph, or hold a book discussion. The activities are designed for a variety of levels of ability, and teachers should choose ones appropriate for their classes.

The units developed for grades four and five demand much more self-directed work. Only a few books are suggested to be read aloud by the teachers. Teachers will introduce the books and children will carry out appropriate activities. Students are encouraged to complete a variety of research activities and accept the responsibility of sharing their findings with the other students. Many of the follow-up activities provide a variety of problem solving and decision-making opportunities. The follow-up activities for individual or small groups may be accomplished with little or no teacher direction. Some of the fourth–fifth grade units are long because it is recognized that the local social studies units at this level will probably be broken down into smaller segments. The number of trade books and activities included should allow needed flexibility.

REFERENCES

1. George W. Maxim, *Social Studies and the Elementary School Child*. (Columbus, OH: Charles E. Merrill, 1983), p. 158.

2. Paul R. Hanna, *Assuring Quality for the Social Studies in Our Schools*. (Stanford: Stanford University, Hoover Institution Press, 1987), p. 5.

3. Maxim, p. 57.

4. Curriculum Task Force of the National Commission on Social Studies in the Schools, *Charting a Course: Social Studies for the 21st Century*. (Washington, DC: National Commission on Social Studies in the Schools, 1989).

5. Christine I. Bennett, *Comprehensive Multicultural Education*. (Boston: Allyn and Bacon, 1990), p. 290.

Chapter 1
Kindergarten/Transition/
First Grade

Myself

STUDENT OBJECTIVES:

1. Point out the physical and behavioral changes that occur by age six.
2. State ways people adjust their behavior in response to changes in weather and seasons.
3. Explain the benefits of a child's accepting responsibility for his/her behavior.
4. Demonstrate why obeying safety rules is necessary to personal well-being.
5. Explain how using the five senses aids in interpreting one's environment.
6. Discuss the importance of developing self-esteem.

RECOMMENDED READINGS:

Borden, Louise. *Caps, Hats, Socks, and Mittens.* Illustrated by Lillian Hoban. Scholastic, 1989.
Simple text and illustrations identify the joyful ways children adjust to the changing seasons. (Objectives 2 and 5)

Carlson, Nancy. *I Like Me!* Viking, 1988.
A young pig thinks about her good traits and decides she likes herself. (Objective 6)

de Paola, Tomie. *Now One Foot, Now the Other.* G. P. Putnam's Sons, 1981.
Grandfather taught Bobby to walk, and later, after Grandfather's stroke, Bobby teaches him to walk. (Objective 3)

Howe, James. *I Wish I Were a Butterfly.* Illustrated by Ed Young. Harcourt Brace Jovanovich, 1987.
A kind spider helps a little cricket regain his self-esteem after the bullfrog hurts his feelings. (Objective 6)

Keller, Holly. *Cromwell's Glasses.* Greenwillow, 1982.
New glasses aid little Cromwell the rabbit, and his family helps him adjust to wearing them. (Objectives 3 and 4)

Kraus, Robert. *Boris Bad Enough.* Illustrated by Jose Aruego and Ariane Dewey. Simon & Schuster, 1976.
Boris's parents find their own actions negatively affect his behavior. (Objectives 3 and 6)

Krauss, Ruth. *The Growing Story.* Illustrated by Phyllis Rowand. Harper & Row, 1947.
A little boy who watches plants and animals grow finally realizes that he is growing too. (Objectives 1 and 2)

Maestro, Betsy and Maestro, Giulio. *Harriet Reads Signs and More Signs.* Crown, 1981.
Harriet reads and uses signs to guide her behavior on her way to Grandmother's house. (Objectives 3 and 4)

Marshall, James. *Goldilocks and the Three Bears.* Dial, 1988.
A rude and irresponsible Goldilocks enters the house of the three bears without an invitation. (Objective 3)

Mayer, Mercer. *When I Get Bigger.* Western, 1983.
Little Critter tells about the things he will be able to do when he gets bigger. (Objective 1)

McCully, Emily Arnold. *New Baby.* Harper & Row, 1988.
In this wordless picture book, a little mouse acts babyish to get attention when a new baby arrives, but he finds being a helper relieves his jealousy. (Objective 3)

Pearson, Susan. *My Favorite Time of Year.* Illustrated by John Wallner. Harper & Row, 1988.
A family gets ready for each approaching season and then adapts its activities to suit the season. (Objective 2)

Stevenson, Sucie. *I Forgot.* Orchard, 1988.
Arthur remembers an important family day after forgetting a number of things. (Objective 3)

Weiss, Nicki. *Barney Is Big.* Greenwillow, 1988.
Barney recalls what he did as a baby and realizes how big he has grown. (Objective 1)

Zolotow, Charlotte. *One Step, Two.* Rev. ed. Illustrated by Cindy Wheeler. Lothrop, Lee & Shepard, 1981.
A little girl uses her senses to point out things her mother misses on their spring walk. (Objectives 2 and 5)

————. *Someone New*. Illustrated by Erik Blegvad. Harper & Row, 1978.
Erik feels someone is missing and discovers that he is growing and developing new interests. (Objective 1)

GROUP INTRODUCTORY ACTIVITY:

Preparation: Locate *The Growing Story* by Ruth Krauss. Ask several parents of students in the class to let you use items of clothing their children wore when they were babies or toddlers.

Focus: Show the baby clothes to the class and allow the students to pass them around. Guide the students to notice the size difference between these clothes and the ones they are wearing. Ask if anyone recognizes any of the clothes. After discussion, reveal the names of the students who previously wore the clothing. Encourage the owners to stand up holding the clothes in front of them to demonstrate how much they have grown.

Objective: To address the objective of pointing out the physical and behavioral changes that occur by age six, say to the class, "Each of you is growing all the time, but you grow so slowly it is almost impossible to notice it is happening. As I read this story, you will discover how one boy noticed he was growing."

Guided Activity: Read Ruth Krauss's *The Growing Story*. Stop with the page describing how summer was ending. Let the class predict how the little boy will find out that he is growing along with the trees and baby animals. Finish the book and discuss how close the predictions came to the actual ending of the story. In which seasons do plants do most of their growing? Do people grow only in certain seasons or do they grow all year round? How does one know? What does it mean to be "grown up?" Are there any benefits to being a child?

Suggest that the students bring a snapshot of themselves when they were younger. Display the photographs on a bulletin board titled "We're Growing Up." See if the children can recognize one another.

Extending Activity: Develop a choral reading of the poem "The End" from A. A. Milne's *Now We Are Six* (E. P. Dutton, 1927). Begin by repeating the poem enough times for the children to memorize it. Vary the voices of the presentation by assigning one line to boys, one to girls, another to a single student, some to the whole class, etc. Practice several times before performing for another class or the principal.

FOLLOW-UP ACTIVITIES FOR TEACHER AND STUDENTS TO SHARE:

1. Before reading Louise Borden's *Caps, Hats, Socks, and Mittens* to the class, tell the students to watch the illustrations and listen to the words in order to discuss how children dress, play, and act in different ways as the seasons change. After the book is read, let the students discuss how children's lives vary in each of the four seasons.

   Divide the chalkboard into four columns titled "In Summer," "In Spring," "In Fall," and "In Winter." Go back through the book and have the students discuss the use of the five senses in each season. As they think of ways sight, hearing, smell, taste, and touch are associated with individual seasons, record their thoughts in the appropriate column. For example, their ideas might include: "In summer pavement feels hot" or "In fall pumpkin pie tastes spicy." Have each student select a sentence to illustrate. Arrange the pictures in a "Four Seasons/Five Senses" book.

2. Introduce Nancy Carlson's *I Like Me!* by asking the children to suggest things they do that cause them to like themselves. Record their answers on butcher paper that has been titled "We Like Ourselves When." Read the story. Talk about the pig's good traits that caused her to like herself. Why is it important to feel good about oneself? If available, place individual pictures of the students on the butcher paper list. If not, take a group picture of the class to attach to the list. Have the students illustrate the border with "I Like Me" ideas.

3. Read aloud Tomie de Paola's *Now One Foot, Now the Other*. Let the children recall things Bobby did to help Grandfather after his stroke. Brainstorm other things children might do to help grandparents or older relatives and neighbors. Suggest that students actually do some of the things brainstormed and report their good deeds to the class.

4. Before reading James Howe's *I Wish I Were a Butterfly*, ask the children to share with the class a time someone hurt their feelings. What did the person say? How did the children react? What did they do to feel better?

   Tell the class that Howe's book is about how a little cricket deals with hurt feelings. Read the story. Ask the children to discuss what the bullfrog said to hurt the little cricket's feelings, how the cricket reacted, and why he began to feel better about himself. How do the children suppose the little cricket felt when he heard the butterfly speak?

As an extending activity, have the children sit in a circle. Ask them to close their eyes and think of some person, animal, or thing they would rather be. Let them take turns saying, "I wish I were a/an _____ ," filling in the blank with their wishes. Let the child on the speaker's right say, "But I'm glad you are you because _____ ," filling in the blank with a compliment. Go around the circle until all have made a wish, received a compliment, and given a compliment.

5. Read Holly Keller's *Cromwell's Glasses* aloud. In what ways did Cromwell's brothers and sisters help him adjust to the new glasses? What might the students do to help family members? Have the children illustrate their favorite helping idea for an "I Can Help" bulletin board.

6. Before reading Robert Kraus's *Boris Bad Enough* let the children talk about why they sometimes behave badly. Tell them this is a story about Boris, whose parents take him to a psychiatrist because of his behavior. After reading the book, refer to the illustrations to talk about what Boris did that was bad behavior. What did the psychiatrist tell the parents? What did each parent do to improve? Why did Boris change his behavior? Have sheets of paper titled "I acted badly when. . . ," and at the bottom "I felt better when. . . ." Let the students illustrate the bad behavior. Record their words about what made them feel better.

7. After reading Betsy and Giulio Maestro's *Harriet Reads Signs and More Signs*, take a camera along on a class walk. Read, photograph, and obey the signs encountered on the walk. When the class returns to school, discuss taking the walk alone as opposed to walking with a group. What would the students have done differently if they had been alone? When the film is developed, make a display of the photographed signs. Read the book again. Did the class see the same signs that Harriet saw? Continue to add to the display with additional photographs and student drawings of signs.

8. To introduce James Marshall's *Goldilocks and the Three Bears*, ask the students to discuss what they think it means to be responsible. How do other people feel about responsible children? After reading the story, ask what irresponsible things Goldilocks did. How did others feel about her? If time allows, read "The Three Bears'" in Tomie de Paola's *Favorite Nursery Rhymes* (G. P. Putnam's Sons, 1986). What other irresponsible things did Goldilocks do in that story? Did the Goldilocks in either story break any laws, e. g., destruction of property,

breaking and entering, etc.? Let children think of some rules of good behavior Goldilocks should have practiced.

9. After reading Mercer Mayer's *When I Get Bigger*, ask the students what things they have already done that Little Critter wants to do when he gets bigger. Let the students think of other things school children do that show they are growing up. Allow the students to demonstrate their accomplishments by acting them out, e. g., "I can tie my shoe," "I can try not to suck my thumb," etc.

10. Introduce Emily McCully's *New Baby* by discussing how the youngest child of a family might feel when a new baby arrives. Let the children "read" the textless book's illustrations. What was the little mouse's first reaction to the baby? What did he finally do to accept responsibility? Make a list of things young children can do to help the family care for a new baby.

11. To introduce Susan Pearson's *My Favorite Time of Year*, make a large circle on butcher paper. Divide the circle into four parts labeled "Spring," "Summer," "Fall," and "Winter." Explain to the students that some people think of time as a circle because the seasons always follow one another in the same order, and, year after year, the cycle is repeated. By knowing which season comes next, people are able to prepare for it.

    Read the book. What did the family do to prepare for each season? What activities did they do in each season because of changing weather conditions? Have students draw small pictures of what they and their families do to get ready for their favorite season. Make a collage of the drawings by pasting them in the appropriate section of the butcher paper circle used to introduce the story.

12. Before class tie a string around your finger. To introduce Sucie Stevenson's *I Forgot*, show the students your finger and explain that tying a string around one's finger is a trick people use to remember something important, and that you used the string to remember to read this book to the class. After reading, let the children discuss the things Arthur did to try to accept the responsibility of remembering. What else might he have done? Ask the students to suggest reasons why he forgot so many things. What made him remember his mother's birthday?

13. Invite several of the students' parents to listen with the class to Nicki Weiss's *Barney Is Big*. After reading, ask the parents to tell the students how they felt when their child went to school for the first time. Let the children also relate their

feelings on the first day of school. How are the parents' and children's feelings the same? How are they different?

14. Read Charlotte Zolotow's *One Step, Two* aloud. Let the students talk about what senses the little girl used to enjoy the things around her. What sense did she *not* use? (taste) What clue did the mother give to let the reader know she will use that sense later? Using older children or parent volunteers, take the students in small groups on a walk. Let them decide how many steps they will take before stopping to use their senses. Have the volunteers record the sensory experiences reported by the students. After returning to school, share the list of things observed. This activity can be extended by taking one walk in the fall and another in the spring and then comparing the two.

15. Read Zolotow's *Someone New* to the class. Let the children identify the things that made Erik discover he was someone new. On butcher paper list the children's suggestions of things they liked before going to school that they do not like now. Title the list "Growing Up." Let students share in illustrating a border for the paper with things they like to do now.

Families

STUDENT OBJECTIVES:

1. Give examples of the varied combinations of people that can make up a household.
2. Identify the terms (nieces, cousins, great aunts, etc.) that indicate members of an extended family.
3. Discuss activities families do for fun and to show love for one another.
4. Discuss ways families can cope with crises and personal problems.

RECOMMENDED READINGS:

Aliki. *The Two of Them.* Greenwillow, 1979.
Grandfather cared for the little girl until she grew up; then she cared for him until his death. (Objectives 1, 3, and 4)

Blaustein, Muriel. *Play Ball, Zachary!* Harper & Row, 1988.
A little tiger and his father have different ideas about how to have fun but learn to enjoy games together. (Objective 3)

Brown, Laurene Krasny and Brown, Marc. *Dinosaurs Divorce.* Little, Brown, 1986.
Lively text and humorous illustrations address the many anxieties a child of divorced parents must face. (Objectives 1, 3, and 4)

Cameron, Ann. *The Stories Julian Tells.* Illustrated by Ann Strugnell. Pantheon, 1981.
Julian tells five stories about life in his family and neighborhood. (Objective 3)

Clifton, Lucille. *Everett Anderson's Goodbye.* Illustrated by Ann Grifalconi. Henry Holt , 1983.
After the death of his father, a little boy goes through the five stages of denial, anger, bargaining, depression, and, finally, acceptance. (Objectives 1 and 4)

Drescher, Joan. *Your Family, My Family.* Walker, 1980.
Shows the value of family love as differing combinations of people who make a family unit are shared. (Objectives 1 and 2)

Fisher, Iris. *Katie-Bo.* Illustrated by Mariam Schaer. Adama, 1987.
The loving story of an American family that adopts a Korean child. (Objective 1)

Hutchins, Pat. *The Very Worst Monster.* William Morrow, 1985.
Hazel finds a way to overcome the jealousy caused by the attention her baby brother receives. (Objective 4)

MacLachlan, Patricia. *Mama One, Mama Two.* Illustrated by Ruth Lercher Bornstein. Harper & Row, 1982.
A little girl lives with foster parents while her mother recovers from mental illness. (Objectives 1 and 4)

Moore, Elaine. *Grandma's House.* Illustrated by Elise Primavera. Lothrop, Lee & Shepard, 1985.
Summer in the country is a special time for both a little girl and her grandmother. (Objectives 2 and 3)

Roy, Ron. *Breakfast with My Father.* Illustrated by Troy Howell. Houghton Mifflin, 1980.
When his father, who is separated from his mother, does not come to take him to Saturday breakfast, David is disappointed. (Objectives 1, 3, and 4)

Rylant, Cynthia. *The Relatives Came.* Illustrated by Stephen Gammell. Bradbury, 1985.
Relatives from Virginia come to visit and share love, laughter, and work in a crowded, but happy, home. (Objectives 2 and 3)

Stock, Catherine. *Sophie's Knapsack*. Lothrop, Lee & Shepard, 1988.
Susie and her parents take an overnight hiking trip to the top of Purple
Cloud Rock. (Objective 3)

GROUP INTRODUCTORY ACTIVITY:

Preparation: Locate *The Stories Julian Tells* by Ann Cameron. Buy
enough packages of instant or cooking-required lemon pudding mix to
serve the class. Consult label directions for utensils and additional
ingredients needed.

Focus: Ask the children to close their eyes and visualize as you say,
"Imagine you are holding a lemon. Hold it close to your nose and
smell it. Pretend you are slicing it in half. Take a big bite. Now open
your eyes and tell me what change has taken place in your mouth."
After the children have shared their responses, say, "The smell and
taste of lemon must be powerful for a simple suggestion to have
created so much saliva in your mouth. Just imagine how much your
mouth would water if you had to sit and look at a delicious lemon
pudding."

Objective: To approach the objective of discussing activities families
do for fun and to show love for one another, say to the children,
"The story I am going to read tells how the smell of lemon caused
Julian and his little brother Huey to disobey their father. Listen to
find out how their father reacted to their misbehavior."

Guided Activity: Before reading "A Pudding Like a Night on the Sea"
from *The Stories Julian Tells*, explain to the students that there are
few pictures in the book and that the author, Ann Cameron, wants
them to use their imaginations to see, hear, taste, and smell the
events of the story. After the reading, ask students how the members
of Julian's family showed kindness to one another. What was special
about Julian's father? How else might he have reacted to the missing
pudding? Ask the students if any member of their families, other than
their mothers, cooks a special food that the whole family likes.

Make lemon pudding with the class. Instant pudding is easy to
prepare; cooked pudding allows students to "whip" and "beat" the
ingredients as Julian and Huey did. Whipped egg whites can be
folded into the cooked pudding.

Julian's mother said the pudding tasted "like a whole raft of
lemons. . .like a night on the sea." Why would this compliment make
Julian's father feel good? While the students are eating their pudding,
ask them to think of other examples of figurative language to complete the sentence, " This pudding tastes like. . . ."

Extending Activity: Ask the students' parents to send the recipe for their family's favorite dish. Make copies of the recipes for a class cookbook. Allow students to decorate the cover and take the book home as a gift for the best cook in their family.

FOLLOW-UP ACTIVITIES FOR TEACHER AND STUDENTS TO SHARE:

1. Before reading Aliki's *The Two of Them* to the class, write the words "Made with Love" on the chalkboard. Tell students the book they are going to hear is about what people do and make for one another "with love." After reading, ask what nice things the grandfather and granddaughter did for one another. How does one know they were friends? What items did the grandfather make? As the students respond, list their responses under the title "Made with Love." Do the students own something handmade by a grandparent or other relative? Add these things to the list. Ask students to bring items to class that have been made by members of their families. Allow time for students to "show and tell." Set up a display titled "Made with Love."

2. Read Muriel Blaustein's *Play Ball, Zachary!* Discuss how Zachary felt when he could not play ball well. How did his father feel? How did they work out ways to have fun together? Let the students discuss things they like to do with their mother or father. Suggest they draw a picture of this activity and/or bring an appropriate family snapshot. Label the pictures with the name of the activity and the student's name to make a bulletin board "I Have Fun with My Parents."

3. Read Laurene and Marc Brown's *Dinosaurs Divorce* to the children. Have them pretend a friend's parents are getting a divorce, and the friend is sad. What did they learn from the book that they can suggest to help the friend feel better? Would they recommend the friend check this book out of the library to share with his/her family? Why, or why not?

4. Arrange for the school counselor to visit the class and talk about the death of a family member. Share Lucille Clifton's *Everett Anderson's Goodbye* as an introduction to the visit. Let the counselor lead the discussion of the book and the topic.

5. Read Joan Drescher's *Your Family, My Family* to the class. Let the students discuss the varied combinations of people that can make a family. In what ways are these families alike? Use coloring books, paper doll books, or a clip-art file to create a collection of paper figures that represent a vari-

ety of family members. Be sure the collection is heterogeneous with multi-racial and multi-generational figures included. Let the students select figures and arrange them as a photograph of a family unit different from their own. Help students tape the "family" to a sheet of paper. With a copy machine, duplicate each student's picture. After each student's picture is made, remove figures from the original for others to use. Students may color and label the family portrait.

6. Before reading *Katie-Bo* by Iris Fisher, ask the class what it means to be adopted. Tell the children that the story they are going to hear is about a family in the United States that adopts a little girl from Korea. Locate the United States and Korea on the globe. Read the book aloud. What preparations did the family make for Katie-Bo's arrival? Why did the family decide on the name Katie-Bo? What else did the mother and father have to do before the judge legally made Katie-Bo a member of the family?

   Invite a parent of an adopted child or a social worker to talk to the class about how parents and children are chosen for one another and what is done to help families adjust to the new member. Allow time for students' questions.

7. Before reading *The Very Worst Monster* by Pat Hutchins, explore with the students reasons why children may be angry with a new baby in the family. As an extension of their comments, discuss the meaning of the word "jealous." After reading the book, ask students what Hazel did to show she was jealous. What made her change and not be so jealous anymore? How could her parents have helped her get over her angry feelings sooner?

8. Before reading Patricia MacLachlan's *Mama One, Mama Two*, display two pictures--a bright one that evokes a happy feeling and a dark one that evokes a sad feeling. If available, Van Gogh's "Sunflowers" and "Potato Eaters" are appropriate. Explain that artists often use bright colors to portray happiness and dark colors to indicate sadness. While reading the book, point out the artwork displayed in the illustrations. After reading, ask the class to identify the meaning of a foster home. Why do children live in foster homes? Why was Maudie content in her foster home? Why did Katherine tell Maudie that spring will be whenever Mama One comes home?

   Let the students finger paint pictures, choosing either "happy" or "sad" as a theme. Be sure both bright and dark colors are available. Display the artwork by category.

9. To introduce Elaine Moore's *Grandma's House*, ask the children if anyone has visited a relative that lives far away. Explain that people often carry special memories back home after such a visit. Read the book to the class. What will the little girl in the story recall as a special memory after she returns home? Do the students have special memories of visiting a grandparent or other relative?

   Encourage students to ask their own parents about childhood visits to grandparents. The next day, allow time for students to share their parents' memories with the class.

10. Before sharing Ron Roy's *Breakfast with My Father*, talk about how children feel when their parents separate. Read the book to the class. Discuss why David was so disappointed when his father did not seem to be coming to take him to breakfast. How did he feel when he saw his father in the kitchen? Brainstorm some things David's family might do to have a good time that weekend.

11. Before reading Cynthia Rylant's *The Relatives Came*, have the children recall all the words they know that name members of their extended families, e.g., cousin, grandfather, aunt, etc. Record their answers on a transparency. After reading the story, go back and let the children examine the illustrations again. Using the overhead transparency as a vocabulary guide, let the students decide what they think the relationships are among the members of the family in the story. How does one know this is a happy family? What activities showed they enjoyed each other? How did the guests help accept responsibility?

    Ask students to bring pictures of their extended families for a "Family Show and Tell." Let each student tell something he or she enjoys doing when relatives visit.

12. Ask the students if they have ever been on a trip with their families. Where did they go? How did they get there? Read aloud Catherine Stock's *Sophie's Knapsack*. What hints did the illustrator give that indicate the family lives in the city? What items did Sophie take on the trip? How did the family share responsibilities while they were camping? What did they eat? What did Sophie take home to remind herself of the trip?

    Let the students plan a pretend overnight trip to a nearby lake, mountain, or beach. What food would they take? What form of transportation would they use? What could they do to have fun while they were there? Ask the students to bring a picture of any overnight trip they may have taken or any natural thing, such as shells, leaves, rocks, etc., they brought back. Make a display of the items they bring.

Economics of Family Living

STUDENT OBJECTIVES:

1. Suggest ways families can earn and spend money appropriately.
2. Describe family activities designed to save money.
3. Categorize family purchases as wants or needs.
4. Discuss how a family's economic circumstances affect behavior.
5. Suggest ways children may contribute to the financial well-being of their families.

RECOMMENDED READINGS:

Blaine, Marge. *Terrible Thing That Happened at Our House.* Illustrated by John Wallner. Parents Magazine, 1975.
By accepting responsibilities, the children help the family adjust to the problems that arise when Mother goes back to work. (Objectives 1, 4, and 5)

Hazen, Barbara Shook. *Tight Times.* Illustrated by Trina Schart Hyman. Viking, 1979.
A family supports one another even though the father has lost his job and the family lives in poverty. (Objectives 1, 3, and 4)

Hutchins, Pat. *You'll Soon Grow into Them, Titch.* Greenwillow, 1983.
When the new baby arrives, Titch has the opportunity to "hand down" his clothes that are too small. (Objectives 2 and 3)

Kraus, Robert. *Another Mouse to Feed.* Illustrated by Jose Aruego and Ariane Dewey. Simon & Schuster, 1980.
Thirty-one little mice find jobs and assume household chores to help their parents support the thirty-second little mouse left on their doorstep. (Objectives 1, 4, and 5)

Rylant, Cynthia. *This Year's Garden.* Illustrated by Mary Szilagyi. Bradbury, 1984.
As the seasons change, so do the family's responsibilities in caring for the garden. (Objectives 2 and 5)

Smith, Miriam. *Annie and Moon.* Illustrated by Lesley Moyes. Gareth Stevens, 1989.
As Moon the cat must adjust to living in a succession of new places, so must Annie and her mother. (Objective 4)

Viorst, Judith. *Alexander, Who Used to Be Rich Last Sunday.* Illustrated by Ray Cruz. Atheneum, 1978.
Given a dollar by his grandparents, Alexander spends it little by little, saving none for the walkie-talkie he really wants. (Objectives 1, 2, and 3)

Williams, Vera B. *A Chair for My Mother.* Greenwillow, 1982.
A family saves money to buy a new chair to replace one lost in a fire. (Objectives 1, 2, 3, 4, and 5)

GROUP INTRODUCTORY ACTIVITY:

Preparation: Locate *A Chair for My Mother* by Vera Williams. Have ready an empty gallon jar, old magazines and catalogs, scissors, paper, watercolor paints, brushes, glue, and strips of posterboard one and a half inches wide.

Focus: Ask if anyone's family has ever collected aluminum cans for recycling. After students have shared their experiences, explain that families can save money by recycling items that are usually thrown away. Hold up a gallon jar and say, "When I got this jar, it had food in it. Now that it is empty, perhaps it can be used for something else. Help me make a list of ways this empty jar can be used." As the students brainstorm, record their ideas.

Objective: In order to examine ways families can earn, spend, and save money appropriately, introduce Vera Williams's *A Chair for My Mother* by saying, "In this story, you will meet a family who recycled a large jar in a useful way. When I finish reading, I shall ask you to tell me about their idea."

Guided Activity: After reading the book, ask how the family used the jar. Add "saving coins" to the list if it was not previously mentioned. Let students discuss the ways each family member contributed to saving for the chair. Was the chair a "want" or a "need"? After the fire, how did the family get furniture? Are there other ways families replace possessions after a fire? (e. g., insurance)
Return to the book. Tell students the author/illustrator used watercolors to paint the pictures. Direct their attention to the way Williams framed each page with motifs that extend the illustrations and story. Let students find and cut out a picture of something they

would like to save for. After pasting the picture on a sheet of paper, students can frame it by painting strips of cardboard employing the motif technique used by Williams. Pictures can be titled "Wants" or "Needs."

Extending Activity: Using recycled materials, students can make banks for saving coins. To make a simple bank, cut a slit in a circular piece of felt and secure it with a rubber band over the mouth of a baby food jar. An elaborate "piggy-bank" can be made by using a plastic 12 ounce soda bottle that has been laid on its side. For the pig's snout, paint the lid pink with black nostrils. Challenge students to use their imaginations to find items at home that can be "recycled" into eyes, ears, and legs. Use a glue gun to attach these "body parts" to the bottle. The teacher can melt a coin slot in the top of each bank with a heated pointed object. Melt a small hole in the bottom of the bottle for inserting a pipe cleaner that can be curled into a pig's tail.

Students may want to read more about Rosa and her family in Vera Williams's *Something Special for Me* (Greenwillow, 1983) and *Music, Music for Everyone* (Greenwillow, 1984).

FOLLOW-UP ACTIVITIES FOR TEACHER AND STUDENTS TO SHARE:

1. Before reading Marge Blaine's *Terrible Thing That Happened at Our House*, ask the children if any adult in their family works at home rather than outside the house. How would their lives be different if that person were not at home all day? Read the book to the class. What were the changes the little girl did not like after her mother went to work outside the home? What responsibilities did the children accept to ease the problem? What is the meaning of the line, "I guess they're a real mother and father after all"?

2. Show the class Barbara Shook Hazen's *Tight Times*. Ask for suggestions why the book was given that title. Read the story aloud. Now can the students tell why the book has that title? Let students list the wants the little boy had because of "tight times." How do they know the family still had love? Which was the most important family need? What could the family do to have fun even though they were poor? Can pets make people feel better when times are difficult?

   Invite a pet store owner to bring a collection of inexpensive pets for children. Before the visit, let the students browse through a collection of books about pet selection and care. The illustrations may suggest questions they will want to ask the pet store owner.

3. Have students volunteer to tell about a time they received or gave hand-me-downs. Read Pat Hutchins's *You'll Soon Grow into Them, Titch*. Let students discuss why families hand down clothes. Why did Titch's father buy him new ones? What other items besides clothes do family members hand down? Can these items be wants as well as needs? Pull items from a box of hand-me-downs. Let students identify each as a "want" or "need" and defend each answer.

4. Before class, make two finger puppets that look like the mouse characters in *Another Mouse to Feed* by Robert Kraus. Puppets can be made from felt cut into isosceles triangles with whiskers and ears added. One puppet should be parent size and the other child size. Read Kraus's book to the students. What responsibilities did the little mice assume to help their parents? As students respond, record their answers, categorizing them as either "Jobs in the Home" or "Jobs outside the Home."

   With the teacher using the larger puppet as Mother or Father and students using the smaller puppet, let the children role-play telling the parent mouse what they would volunteer to do to help the family cope with the new baby's arrival.

5. Show the students the contents of several vegetable seed packets. Discuss how many vegetables could come from each packet. Point out that some seeds, like carrots and radishes, produce one vegetable. Others, like tomatoes and beans, produce many vegetables per seed. Note the price of the seed packets. Read Cynthia Rylant's *This Year's Garden*. Carefully examine the pictures and discuss the responsibilities of the children during each season. List specific jobs the children did. What happened to the food after it was picked? What can children do to help adults preserve food?

   Arrange a field trip to a grocery store. Compare the price of seeds to the price of the same foods for sale in the store. Which costs families more money, buying food or growing food? Ask the grocer to talk to the students about packaging and shipping of produce. Where is the fresh food grown? How is it kept fresh while it is being transported and while it is in the store?

6. Before reading Miriam Smith's *Annie and Moon*, ask the class to suggest reasons why people move. In two columns on the chalkboard, list each response as a "happy" reason or a "sad" reason. When the story is finished, ask what problems their lack of money caused for Annie and her mother? In what ways were the problems of Moon like those of

Annie and her mother? Can the students now add to the lists of reasons why people move?

7. Using an overhead projector, transparent plastic coins, and a dollar bill, show various combinations of coins that equal a dollar. Leave the projector on, with six dimes, six nickles, and ten pennies displayed; at the same time read Judith Viorst's *Alexander, Who Used to Be Rich Last Sunday.* Each time Alexander says, "Good-bye fifteen cents," "Good-bye four cents," etc., remove coins representing the amount of money spent.

   After the reading, ask students to share a time when they had an experience similar to Alexander's. How does it feel to have money one day and nothing the next? Did Alexander "need" any of his purchases? Ask the students to suggest ways Alexander could discipline himself to save money. List the responses on the chalkboard and discuss the merits of each. As a follow-up, arrange a field trip to a bank to learn about savings accounts.

Homes

STUDENT OBJECTIVES:

1. Analyze how climate, environment, and special wants and needs determine how homes are built, decorated, and furnished.
2. Recognize that the layout of rooms, houses, and neighborhoods can be drawn into floorplans and maps.
3. Define terms used in house construction and maintenance.
4. Identify specific types of houses and name the rooms within.
5. Discuss why people move and what adjustments must be made.

RECOMMENDED READINGS:

Asch, Frank. *Goodbye House.* Prentice-Hall, 1986.
   Baby Bear feels ready to move after his family helps him say goodbye. (Objective 5)

Barton, Byron. *Building a House.* Greenwillow, 1980.
Briefly identifies types of workers involved in building a house. (Objectives 3 and 4)

Brandenberg, Franz. *Aunt Nina and Her Nephews and Nieces.* Illustrated by Aliki. Greenwillow, 1983.
Aunt Nina invites her nephews and nieces to her cat's birthday party. (Objective 4)

Gibbons, Gail. *Tool Book.* Holiday House, 1982.
Identifies the tools used in building and maintaining a house and illustrates the purpose of each. (Objective 3)

Greenfield, Eloise. *Grandmama's Joy.* Illustrated by Carole Byard. Philomel, 1980.
Grandmama is sad because the family must move, but Rhondy reminds her that she is "Grandmama's joy." (Objective 5)

Hoberman, Mary Ann. *A House Is a House for Me.* Illustrated by Betty Fraser. Viking, 1978.
Explores the concept of "house" by identifying the houses of animals and objects. (Objective 4)

Hogner, Franz. *From Blueprint to House.* Carolrhoda, 1986.
Introduces many terms as the step-by-step building of a house occurs. (Objectives 2 and 3)

Maynard, Joyce. *New House.* Illustrated by Steve Bethel. Harcourt Brace Jovanovich, 1987.
Andy builds a tree house as he observes the construction of a new house down the road. (Objective 3)

Mendoza, George. *Need a House? Call Ms. Mouse!* Illustrated by Doris Susan Smith. Grosset & Dunlap, 1981.
Henrietta Mouse designs and decorates appropriate homes for her animal friends. (Objective 1)

100 Words about My House. Illustrated by Richard Brown. Harcourt Brace Jovanovich, 1988.
Items found in various areas in and around the house are illustrated and labeled. (Objectives 1 and 4)

Pinkwater, Daniel Manus. *The Big Orange Splot.* Hastings House, 1977.
Houses on the street change in appearance as each owner paints his dreams. (Objective 1)

Roth, Harold. *Let's Look All Around the House.* Grosset & Dunlap, 1988.
Children may lift flaps to discover items that can be found behind closed doors in ordinary homes. (Objective 1)

Schertle, Alice. *In My Treehouse.* Illustrated by Meredith Dunham. Lothrop, Lee & Shepard, 1983.
A child shares the joys of owning a treehouse. (Objective 2)

Zemach, Margot. *The Three Little Pigs.* Farrar, Straus and Giroux, 1988.

In the traditional story, three pig brothers build houses of different materials. (Objective 1)

GROUP INTRODUCTORY ACTIVITY:

Preparation: Locate *Need a House? Call Ms. Mouse!* by George Mendoza. Collect a variety of out-dated paint, wallpaper, fabric, and carpet samples. Cut for each student a piece of poster board that measures approximately 11 by 14 inches.

Focus: Write the word "decorate" on the board. Ask students what they think the word means. Guide the discussion to include words associated with home decoration: color, paint, wallpaper, carpet, furniture, etc. Ask, "Why are all homes not decorated the same?" Lead students to explore the concept that personality, taste, and special needs influence the decoration of homes.

Objective: In order to consider how special wants and needs determine the way homes are built, decorated, and furnished, direct the students' attention to the illustration on the cover of George Mendoza's *Need a House? Call Ms. Mouse!* Before reading point out the drawing table, sketches, and overflowing waste basket. Say, "I can tell from the crumpled paper that Ms. Mouse is trying and trying again to get each drawing just right. While I read, look carefully at the houses Ms. Mouse designs and decorates. Think of ways each home is 'just right' for its owner. We will discuss your ideas after completing the book."

Guided Activity: After reading, examine selected illustrations with the students. Why is each house particularly well-designed for its owner? Place the book in the class library for students to examine independently.

Let students examine a collection of decorator samples. Encourage students to use vocabulary typical of home decoration—drapes, floor covering, wallpaper, etc. Share the unique names manufacturers give to shades of similar colors and to fabric and wallpaper designs. Show samples of paint, wallpaper, fabric, and carpet that might go well together. Let students choose and cut out samples they would like to have in their rooms at home. The carpet pieces will need to be cut by the teacher. Have them glue their selections to a piece of poster board.

When students have finished, let them title their grouping with one of the fanciful names the manufacturers used for their designs. Allow time for students to show and talk about their choices.

Extending Activity: Take the class to visit the interior designer at a local furniture store. Ask the designer to tell the students how she or he helps decorate a home to suit the taste and special needs of family members. If a museum is available locally, the teacher may also want to take the class to see displays of historical and/or miniature rooms.

FOLLOW-UP ACTIVITIES FOR TEACHER AND STUDENTS TO SHARE:

1. Before reading Frank Asch's *Goodbye House*, ask if any students have ever moved from one house to another. How did they feel about leaving? Why? If they felt sad, how were they able to get over the unhappy feeling? Read the book to the class. How did Baby Bear feel as the story began? What did his parents do to make him feel better?

2. After reading aloud Byron Barton's *Building a House*, review the illustrations. From the side and front view of the house on the title page, let students decide if it is one or two stories high, documenting their reasons. While examining the pictures, talk about the job name for each person. Decide in what room the plumber is installing pipes. From scrutinizing the illustrations, let students discuss what rooms are probably in the house.

   Invite a plumber to the class. In addition to bringing tools and pipe fittings for the students to examine, the plumber can demonstrate the use of the tools and talk about a plumber's responsibility in building a house. Have students prepare a list of questions for the plumber to answer.

3. Read Franz Brandenberg's *Aunt Nina and Her Nephews and Nieces* aloud. What rooms did the students see in the illustrations of Aunt Nina's house? Do all houses have a basement and an attic? To what use did Aunt Nina put these rooms? Why did she keep the animals in the basement? Sketch a large outline of a house on the chalkboard. Include a basement below ground level and an attic. Ask students to suggest ways basements and attics can be used. Write their ideas on the appropriate part of the house.

4. Share the first page of Gail Gibbons's *Tool Book* with the class. See how many of the illustrated tools the children can identify. Read the book, talking about the use of each. When finished, turn to the first page and see how many tools the children can name now. Let them tell how each is used—to measure, to pound, etc. Have the children check the tools they have at home. As the children report their findings, list and tally the tools they name. From the tally,

make a bar graph that shows which tools are most commonly used in the children's homes.

5. Read Eloise Greenfield's *Grandmama's Joy* to the class. Why was Grandmama sad? What did Rhondy do to try to cheer her up? Let the students discuss reasons why people move. When can it be a happy rather than a sad experience? How can children help when the family moves?

6. Ask the students in what special house a bird lives. Do cars have houses? Do ears have houses? Explain that Mary Ann Hoberman's *A House Is a House for Me* has ideas about special houses for things. After reading the book let the students examine the illustrations, identifying the unique name for each house and classifying each as a house for animals, people, or objects. Record responses on an overhead transparency that has been divided into three columns. Encourage students to think of possibilities that have not been included in Hoberman's book.

   Let the students choose a house and its occupant from the list to illustrate. Help students label and classify their drawings as houses for people, animals, or objects. Allow time for sharing their drawings.

7. Read aloud Franz Hogner's *From Blueprint to House*. Have students think of the new words they learned from the book. Write each response with a marker on a large index card and discuss the meaning of the word. Guide the discussion to include all important steps in house building. With clothes pins, clip the cards to a clothes line. After all cards are displayed, have students suggest the start-to-finish order of steps in the process of building a house. Rearrange the cards in sequential order and explain that the class has created a timeline.

8. Write the words "builder," "carpenter," "electrician," "plumber," "insulator," "mason," "sheetrocker," and "painter" on the chalkboard. Read the words and ask the students to explain what a person with each occupation does. Put question marks by the ones students are unable to define. Before reading *New House* by Joyce Maynard, tell the students that all the workers listed will appear in the story.

   After reading the book, ask about the occupations with question marks. Review the illustrations of special equipment used by the workers. Let the children build with scrap lumber obtained at a construction site or lumber yard.

9. Before sharing *100 Words about My House*, label the chalkboard with the areas illustrated in the book. Share the

book, showing the illustrations and letting the students identify the object. When they cannot identify an object, encourage them to look at the first letter of its name and guess, based on the beginning sound. When the class has gone through the book, ask them to recall objects found in each area. Record their responses under the appropriate label on the chalkboard. Share the illustrations again and record the forgotten objects they can now recall.

Discuss with the class which rooms or areas illustrated in the book are not in their own homes. What areas or rooms do they have in their homes that the illustrator did not include in the book? Add these to the chalkboard and list items found in these areas or rooms.

10. Have students close their eyes and visualize their own homes. Ask them to think of changes they would like to make in their homes and to visualize those changes. Briefly share ideas. Read Daniel Manus Pinkwater's *The Big Orange Splot*. Talk about the dream of each homeowner.

Duplicate for each student a picture of a plain house similar to the original ones on Mr. Plumbean's street. Let the students use their imaginations to decorate the house so that it looks "like all their dreams." Line the pictures along the chalk tray as if it were a street. Would neighbors who lived in plain houses object to houses that are decorated this way?

11. Share Harold Roth's *Let's Look All Around the House* using a four step method: (1) read the text, (2) let the class predict what items will be found behind the flap, (3) ask a child to open the flap to reveal the picture, and (4) see which of the anticipated items was actually illustrated by Roth. What storage areas are shown in the book? Are there any others that could have been included? Give children old magazines from which to cut out an item found in a house. After they glue the selected item on paper, tape a construction paper flap over the item and label it. Use these to make a class *Let's Look All Around the House* book.

12. Take the class outside under a tree to listen to Alice Schertle's *In My Treehouse*. When the story is finished, ask the children to pretend there is a house in the tree they are sitting under. What activities might children enjoy there? If the students had a treehouse view of the school yard and the immediate neighborhood, what would they see? Let the students climb on the jungle gym to get an overview of the area. Ask them to imagine this overview as a map like the one in the book. Back in the classroom, follow the students' directions as you draw a simple map of the school yard and

surrounding neighborhood as viewed from the imaginary treehouse.

13. Before reading Margot Zemach's *The Three Little Pigs*, ask students to list the kinds of materials houses can be made of. Record their responses. Why do people choose those materials? Now read the story. Why was the house made of straw not a good idea? Which house was best? Why? Can the children think of any house-building materials to add to the list? Let the children work together in small groups to build a house of wood, clay, straw, cardboard, or other available material. Make a display of their work.

Children and Their Families Near and Far

STUDENT OBJECTIVES:

1. Discuss the variety of cultural backgrounds and the way of life of children in various parts of the United States.
2. Analyze how weather and special needs affect the clothing and shelter of families outside the United States.
3. Identify characteristic foods of various cultures.
4. Discuss ways families around the world are similar.
5. Locate on a globe the students' home and the countries of the specific families studied.

RECOMMENDED READINGS:

Aardema, Verna. *Bringing the Rain to Kapiti Plain.* Illustrated by Beatriz Vidal. Dial, 1981.
A Nandi tale of how Ki-pat brings rain to end the drought is told in a cumulative rhyme. (Objectives 2 and 5)

Allen, Thomas B. *Where Children Live.* Prentice-Hall, 1980.
Illustrations and brief text describe the way of life of 13 children around the world. (Objectives 1, 2, 4, and 5)

Daly, Niki. *Not So Fast, Songololo.* Atheneum, 1985.
Gogo takes her grandson Malusi shopping and buys him a new pair of shoes. (Objectives 2, 4, and 5)

de Paola, Tomie. *Watch Out for the Chicken Feet in Your Soup.* Prentice-Hall, 1974.
Joey is embarrassed to introduce Eugene to his Italian grandmother, but he appreciates her in a new way when his friend likes her. (Objectives 1 and 3)

Factor, June. *Summer.* Illustrated by Alison Lester. Viking, 1988.
In Australia, the family celebrates Christmas in summer with special foods and activities. (Objectives 3, 4, and 5)

Greenfield, Eloise. *Honey, I Love.* Illustrated by Diane and Leo Dillon. Thomas Y. Crowell, 1972.
A young African-American girl shares poems of activities and people she loves and enjoys. (Objectives 1 and 4)

Haskins, Jim. *Count Your Way through Japan.* Illustrated by Martin Skoro. Carolrhoda, 1987.
Using the Japanese words and symbols for numbers one through ten, concepts about life in Japan are presented. (Objectives 1, 2, 4, and 5)

Levinson, Riki. *Watch the Stars Come Out.* Illustrated by Diane Goode. E. P. Dutton, 1985.
Grandma tells the little girl about her mother's long trip to America by boat to join her family. (Objectives 1 and 5)

Martin, Bill, Jr. and Archambault, John. *Knots on a Counting Rope.* Illustrated by Ted Rand. Henry Holt, 1987.
An American Indian boy and his grandfather recall his birth, his horse, and an amazing race. (Objectives 1 and 4)

Pomerantz, Charlotte. *The Chalk Doll.* Illustrated by Frane Lessac. J. B. Lippincott, 1989.
Rosa's mother describes her childhood in Jamaica. (Objectives 2, 4, and 5)

Rogers, Jean. *Runaway Mittens.* Illustrated by Rie Munoz. Greenwillow, 1988.
A little Eskimo boy is always losing his mittens until newborn puppies put them to use. (Objectives 1, 4, and 5)

Say, Allen. *The Bicycle Man.* Houghton Mifflin, 1982.
A group of Japanese school children and their parents are amazed by an American soldier's bicycle tricks. (Objective 4)

Weston, Reiko. *Cooking the Japanese Way.* Lerner, 1983.
Shares food habits and recipes of the Japanese people. (Objective 3)

GROUP INTRODUCTORY ACTIVITY:

Preparation: Locate *Where Children Live* by Thomas Allen. Have ready a globe, transparent tape, and 13 slips of paper with the names Rosa, Nils, Hans, Jake, Ivan, Mimi, Nanu, Siwa, Coleen, Majida, Dan, Obi, and Turi written on them.

Focus: Show students the globe and explain that children live in almost every land area shown there. Point out the cold regions near the North Pole, the tropical areas near the equator, and the desert and temperate regions in between. Say, "People all over the world are alike in many ways, but because of differences in the places where they live they sometimes dress and live in ways that are unusual to us."

Objective: To analyze how weather and special needs affect families outside the United States, to note how families around the world are similar, and to begin to share diverse cultural backgrounds within the United States, tell the students that in Thomas Allen's *Where Children Live* they will meet 13 children who all live in different places. Ask them to think about climate regions in order to make educated guesses about the way of life of each child.

Guided Activity: Tell students the first child they will meet is Rosa. She lives in Nicaragua. Tape the slip of paper with her name on the country. Can any student guess about the weather in Rosa's country? What kind of clothes might she wear? What might her house be like? Read about Rosa and then ask students to assess how accurate their predictions were. In what way might Rosa's parents earn a living in their part of Nicaragua? Continue in the same manner for each child in the book until there are 13 names taped to various countries on the globe. How are the 13 children alike? Summarize what has been discussed about how climate affects the way people live.

Extending Activity: See if the library has any illustrated books about the countries discussed. According to the number of books available, divide the students into small groups. Allow time for them to look at their book's illustrations before letting them "show and tell" something interesting they learned about the country.

FOLLOW-UP ACTIVITIES FOR TEACHER AND STUDENTS TO SHARE:

1. Using an overhead or opaque projector, make a poster-size map of Africa, including the country of Kenya. Show the map and tell the students that the people in Verna Aardema's *Bringing the Rain to Kapiti Plain* live in the country of Kenya on the continent of Africa. While reading the book aloud, urge the students to join in as they feel comfortable with the repetition. After the story is read, examine the illustrations of the family's home and clothing. What do these pictures tell us about the climate in that part of Africa? Show the illustration that accompanies the text: "So the grass grew green and the cattle fat." What does it tell about the way of life of the Nandi tribe? Show the next page. What animals besides cattle live on the Kapiti Plain?

Let students draw pictures of African animals. Have them place their pictures around the map of Africa with pieces of yarn connecting the pictures to the country of Kenya.

2. Locate South Africa on the globe and tell students that it is the setting for Niki Daly's *Not So Fast, Songololo*. Before reading the book, ask the children to listen for new words and notice similarities or differences between Songololo's life and theirs. After reading the book, allow students to review the illustrations. What things in South Africa are like they are in the United States, e. g., toy stores, buses, old cans along the sidewalk, etc.? Are there any differences? Hopefully students will notice the word "tackies" and Morris cars as differences. Why might the man in the shoe store be wearing a shirt with U.S.A on it?

3. Before class make a bread doll using the recipe in the back of Tomie de Paola's *Watch Out for the Chicken Feet in Your Soup*. Read the Introduction to the students. Talk about why Joey is embarrassed of his grandmother. After reading, ask the children to discuss why Joey was no longer embarrassed of his grandmother at the end of the story. Will the boys visit her again? Why or why not? Share the bread doll with the students and show them the recipe in the book. Encourage them to check the book out of the library so they can share the bread doll recipe with their families.

4. Locate Australia, the equator, and the United States on the globe. Ask students if they can think of a reason why Australia is nicknamed "the Land Down Under." Explain that seasons are opposite north and south of the equator. Ask students to remember this seasonal difference as you read June Factor's *Summer*. In what ways are the Australian and American Christmas celebrations alike? What are the differences? How does the weather affect this difference? What foods are the same even though the names are different? How are farms in Australia and the United States similar and different? Give each student an outline map of Australia. Let them draw the thing they remember most about the country. Place the map-pictures on a bulletin board titled "Australia, the Land Down Under."

5. Read the first poem in Eloise Greenfield's *Honey, I Love*. Let students recall what the girl loved. Do they love those things too? How do they feel about going to bed? Read "Keepsake." Discuss things the students have that they will never spend or use. Why? Read "Riding on a Train." What did the little girl see that can also be seen riding in a car?

Does riding make the students sleepy? Read "Moochie." Do the students play peek-a-boo with young children? Why do they? Read "By Myself." Let students think of things they would pretend to be if they closed their eyes. With Greenfield's poem as a pattern, write a class poem using the students suggestions. Close the activity with a discussion of how all children are alike.

6. Before reading *Count Your Way through Japan* by Jim Haskins, show students Japan on the globe. Let them share things they already know about the country. Read the book. Ask students what they learned about Japan that they did not know before. How is Japan like the United States? How is it different? Talk about things we own that were made in Japan. Let students bring small items made in Japan. Display the items in sequenced groups numbered one to ten. Label each grouping with the Japanese symbol for the number. If someone in the community does calligraphy, ask them to demonstrate their skill for the children as an example of a similarity between the two countries.

    Study the adult introduction to the food of Japan in Reiko Weston's *Cooking the Japanese Way*. Share ideas about the food that would be of interest to the students. Show the map of Japan in the book and point out the kinds of food pictured. Talk about the food and share the illustrations. If there is someone in the community who is Japanese, ask her/him to talk to the class about their food and customs. Make *mame gohan* or one of the other simple recipes for the children to taste.

7. Point out Europe and North America on the globe. Ask students to think of ways people can travel from one to the other. Tell the students Riki Levinson's *Watch the Stars Come Out* is about a girl and her brother who made the trip on a ship. Read the story. When they arrived in the United States, what was the first thing they saw? How long did the trip take? Why did the doctor examine her thoroughly? Why was the book named *Watch the Stars Come Out?*

    Tell the students that people have come to the United States from all over the world. Show on the globe some of the homelands of American immigrants, such as Africa, Mexico, and the Bering Strait. Have students discuss the various modes of transportation immigrants may have used to get to the United States.

8. Invite an older student to share in reading the two-voice text of *Knots on a Counting Rope* by Bill Martin, Jr. and John Archambault. Ask the class to listen carefully because you will want them to retell the story. Show the picture of

the boy and his grandfather sitting by the campfire to acquaint the class with the setting. Read the story. Then show the students the illustrations and let them take turns telling the story. What did the grandfather mean when he said,"You were born with a dark curtain in front of your eyes"? Why was the boy named Strength of Blue Horses? Ask the students to share a story a grandparent or parent told them about when they were very young.

9. Locate Jamaica on the globe. Tell the children that in Charlotte Pomerantz's *The Chalk Doll* Rosa's mother tells Rosa about her life in Jamaica as a child. Read the story. Talk about how the warm weather affected what the little girl wore in Jamaica. How was her birthday alike and different from the ones the students have? Why was the book called *The Chalk Doll*? Has anyone ever seen a "Raggedy Ann" or homemade rag doll? If any students have a rag doll, ask them to bring it to school for a display.

10. On a globe point out Alaska and the state (if not Alaska) where the students live. Explain that the United States is a big country and not all the states are connected to one another. From its location have the students predict the climate in Alaska. Read Jean Rogers's *Runaway Mittens*. Ask students to describe Pica's clothing. How did his clothes help him live in Alaska's cold climate? Discuss how Pica's family and the students' families live differently. Now discuss ways in which the families are alike. Let the class suppose they were writing a letter to Pica. Record what they would say to him.

11. After reading Allen Say's *The Bicycle Man* aloud, let the students discuss how the Japanese children prepared for their sportsday. What contests did they have? What foods did they eat? In what ways was their sportsday like a field day you might have at your school? Did the Japanese children feel friendly toward the Americans after the soldiers visited? Why? What questions might the children have asked the soldiers if they could have spoken the language?

Friendship

STUDENT OBJECTIVES:

1. Discuss how helpfulness, kindness, good manners, and responsible behavior maintain friendships.
2. Explain how to make new friends.
3. Suggest ways to rebuild friendships that have been damaged.
4. Identify values of cross-generational friendships.
5. Describe how friendships between the disabled and those who are not disabled can benefit both.

RECOMMENDED READINGS:

Aliki. *We Are Best Friends.* Greenwillow, 1982.
  After being lonely when his best friend moves away, Robert makes a new friend. (Objective 2)

Blegvad, Lenore. *Rainy Day Kate.* Illustrated by Erik Blegvad. Macmillan, 1987.
  When Kate can't come to play, her friend makes a pretend Kate to play with. (Objective 1)

Cohen, Miriam. *It's George.* Illustrated by Lillian Hoban. Greenwillow, 1988.
  The other first grade students do not appreciate George until he becomes a hero. (Objectives 1, 4, and 5)

Henriod, Lorraine. *Grandma's Wheelchair.* Illustrated by Christa Chavalier. Albert Whitman, 1982.
  Thomas's grandmother is in a wheelchair so he helps her each morning. (Objectives 4 and 5)

Hurd, Edith Thacher. *I Dance in My Red Pajamas.* Illustrated by Emily Arnold McCully. Harper & Row, 1982.
  Jenny visits her grandparents and all three have a happy, noisy day. (Objective 4)

Joslin, Sesyle. *What Do You Say, Dear?* Illustrated by Maurice Sendak. Young Scott, 1958.
  Humorous situations set the stage for responses about the mannerly thing to say. (Objective 1)

Lasker, Joe. *Nick Joins In.* Albert Whitman, 1980.
  Nick, who cannot walk, is worried about going to school, but finds he can make friends and accept responsibility. (Objectives 1 and 5)

MacLachlan, Patricia. *Through Grandpa's Eyes.* Illustrated by Deborah Ray. Harper & Row, 1980.
A boy uses his senses to interpret the world around him as his grandfather, who is visually impaired, does. (Objectives 4 and 5)

Mueller, Virginia. *A Playhouse for Monster.* Illustrated by Lynn Munsinger. Albert Whitman, 1985.
Selfish monster finds that a playhouse without a playmate with whom to share it is no fun. (Objective 3)

Prelutsky, Jack. *Rolling Harvey Down the Hill.* Illustrated by Victoria Chess. Greenwillow, 1980.
Poems about four children who live in the same apartment house and call themselves friends. (Objective 1)

Rupprecht, Siegfried P. *The Tale of the Vanishing Rainbow.* Illustrated by Jozef Wilkon. North-South Books, 1989.
The bears and wolves almost go to war over the missing rainbow until they learn the value of their longtime friendship. (Objectives 1 and 3)

Udry, Janice May. *Let's Be Enemies.* Illustrated by Maurice Sendak. Harper & Row, 1961.
James and John are friends until bad manners almost ruin the friendship. (Objectives 1 and 3)

Viorst, Judith. *If I Were in Charge of the World.* Illustrated by Lynne Cherry. Atheneum, 1981.
Includes a poem entitled "Since Hanna Moved Away," about a friend who moves. (Objective 2)

Winthrop, Elizabeth. *Lizzie and Harold.* Illustrated by Martha Weston. Lothrop, Lee & Shepard, 1986.
Lizzie wants a best friend but at first thinks it must be a girl. (Objective 2)

GROUP INTRODUCTORY ACTIVITY:

Preparation: Locate *Rainy Day Kate* by Lenore Blegvad. Collect pillows and clothes to make the "Rainy Day Kate" described in the book.

Focus: The book can be introduced by humorously discussing the common childhood problem of boredom. The teacher might want to relate the Introduction to his/her own childhood. she or he can say, "When I was a child and could find no friend to play with, I would put on a sad face and say to my mother, 'I don't have anything to do.' Have you ever said that?" Accept student responses and continue, "I expected her to think of something exciting for me to do, but usually she said, 'Why don't you clean your room.' That was not what I wanted to hear!"

Objective: To approach the objective of how helpfulness, kindness, good manners, and responsible behavior maintain friendships, ask for the students' ideas about how to get over the lonely feeling of having no friend with whom to play. Tell them *Rainy Day Kate* is about a boy who invents a clever solution to the problem. Ask students to listen and find out what he did.

Guided Activity: After reading Blegvad's story, ask students what the boy planned that he and Kate would do to have fun when Kate came to visit? How did he get over his disappointment when Kate could not come because of the rain?

Using pillows and suitable clothes, help the students make a "Rainy Day Kate." What pretend game might they play with her? Would the students like to make a similar doll at home? How might she be like a friend? If the students do make a "Rainy Day Kate" at home, ask them to take her picture and bring the photograph to share with the class.

Extending Activity: Put "Rainy Day Kate" in the classroom's reading area. Let her remain there for the duration of the friendship unit, incorporating her into the activities whenever possible. Suggest the students take turns showing her books and telling her stories during free time. After teaching introduction techniques, let the students practice the skill by introducing her to the principal. Take photographs of the students interacting with her and put them in a scrapbook. At the end of the unit share the scrapbook with the students, using the pictures as a focus for summarizing the concepts learned.

FOLLOW-UP ACTIVITIES FOR TEACHER AND STUDENTS TO SHARE:

1. Before reading Aliki's *We Are Best Friends,* ask the children if any of them has ever had a best friend move away. How did they feel? How did they make new friends? After reading the book aloud, let students discuss why Robert did not at first make friends with Will. What did Robert do to start a friendship with Will? Have students discuss why Robert drew an empty birdcage on his last letter to Peter. What else might he have drawn around the letter? Duplicate a copy of Peter's letter for each child and let them decorate it with pictures related to the story. Suggest they take the letter home and tell the story to their families.

2. Read Miriam Cohen's *It's George.* Let students discuss why the first graders did not make friends with George. Why is it fortunate George made friends with Mr. Emmons? What are George's qualities that make him a good friend to have? When Mr. Emmons gets better, what are some things he and George might do together? What differences between

George and Mr. Emmons make their friendship unusual?
Have the students brainstorm other unusual friendship pairs
and select one pair to illustrate.

3. Before reading Lorraine Henriod's *Grandma's Wheelchair,*
ask students to think of ways young children can help their
grandparents or older neighbors. In what ways can old
people help young children? After reading the story, discuss
the ways Thomas helps his grandmother. In what ways does
their friendship help Jamie also? Visit a nursing home and
let the children make friends with some elderly persons who
live there. Ask the residents to tell the children stories or
teach them songs from their childhood. The class can act
out a favorite story for their cross-generational friends.

4. Read to the class Edith Thacher Hurd's *I Dance in My Red
Pajamas.* Why did Jenny's parents warn her to be quiet? In
what noisy ways did Jenny and her grandparents have fun?
Has anyone in the class stayed overnight with a grandparent? What did they do to have fun? Would the other children like to have a grandparent live nearby? Why is it fun
to make friends with an older person?

5. As you read Sesyle Joslin's *What Do You Say, Dear?* aloud,
let students anticipate the well-mannered answer to "What
do you say, Dear?" before turning the page. Discuss why
each response is appropriate. What are some reasons to use
good manners with friends and family? Let the children play
out their favorite situations from the book.

   Seslye Joslin and Maurice Sendak teamed to do a second etiquette book called *What Do You Do, Dear?* (Young
Scott, 1961) that teachers may also want to share with
children.

6. Read to the class Joe Lasker's *Nick Joins In.* Let the children discuss the fears Nick had as he went to school. How
did the other students help Nick? How did he help them?
Let the children think of another scene that might have
happened to show that Nick had joined in.

7. Before reading Patricia MacLachlan's *Through Grandpa's
Eyes* offer the students an experience that requires them to
identify objects using any one of the four senses other than
the sense of sight. A sound effects tape, or a "feely box"
with a small object inside, or a "scratch and sniff" sticker
will do. Read the book. Ask students to identify ways John
used his senses of touch, smell, and hearing to "see" as
Grandpa did. Let a child volunteer to be blindfolded for
five minutes. During that time let the child report on things

going on around the room by using his/her other senses as Grandpa does.

8. Let students help read the almost textless picture book *A Playhouse for Monster* by Virginia Mueller. How did Monster hurt his friend's feelings? How did he rebuild the friendship? Encourage students to think of other ways Monster could have rebuilt the damaged friendship. Have one member of the class pretend to be the sad rejected child and another pretend to be Monster. Let these and other pairs of students act out a variety of solutions to the problem of rebuilding friendships.

9. Introduce Jack Prelutsky's *Rolling Harvey Down the Hill* by reading the first poem about the boy's four friends. Read the poem again, this time telling the students to listen carefully and select the friend they would most like to have. Let the students vote on the favorite friend, each student giving reasons for his/her choice. Now read "Harvey Always Wins" and "Harvey Never Shares." What things does Harvey do to show he is not kind and helpful? Now read "Tony and the Quarter." Even though the boys were disappointed at the end of the poem, why did the boy say Tony was still his friend?

10. Before reading Siegfried Rupprecht's *The Tale of the Vanishing Rainbow,* tell the students this is a story about friends who almost go to war because they blame each other unfairly. After reading the book, discuss the kind acts the wolves and bears did for each other when they were friends. What caused them to almost go to war without a good reason? At the end of the story what did the bears and wolves do to remember the wise old bear who urged them to remain friends?

    Have students brainstorm words that are characteristic of friendship, e.g., trust, kindness, helpfulness. Have students make construction paper flowers in the colors of the rainbow. Let them chose a "friendship word" to write in the center of their flowers. Make "A Rainbow Garden of Friendship" along the top of the chalkboard to remind the class of the story about the value of preserving friendships that have been made.

11. Have the students share with the class a time their feelings were hurt by a friend. To prepare for reading Janice May Udry's *Let's Be Enemies,* ask students to listen for the bad manners James showed that almost ruined his friendship with John. After reading the story, let students recall James's actions. What happened to make them friends

again? Have students brainstorm other endings for the story. Close by summarizing the ideas, emphasizing the ones that suggest ways of rebuilding damaged friendships.

12. To introduce "Since Hanna Moved Away" from Judith Viorst's *If I Were in Charge of the World,* write on the chalkboard, "When a friend moves away, I feel. . . ." Have the students think of ways to complete the sentence. Then tell them to listen to the poem for examples of how the friend felt when Hanna moved. After reading, ask how the ice cream tasted. What color did the sky seem to be? Now write on the board, "I can make new friends by. . . ." To complete the sentence, have students recall what they did to make new friends when their old friends moved away.

13. Encourage the children to discuss what it means to be a best friend. Do best friends have to be the same age? Must girls only have girls and boys only have boys for best friends? Explain that in Elizabeth Winthrop's *Lizzie and Harold* Lizzie wants a best friend. After reading, ask what made Lizzie finally decide she wanted Harold for a best friend. Discuss what games best friends might play. Acquire enough string so that the class can divide into pairs and learn "Cat's Cradle" and "The Mattress" as described in the book.

Groups: Working and Playing Together

STUDENT OBJECTIVES:

1. List the groups to which a child may belong and examine the values of each.
2. Explain the benefits and responsibilities of working together as a team.
3. Discuss a child's responsibility as a citizen.
4. Describe the tools and services of various adult helper groups.

RECOMMENDED READINGS:

Blacker, Terence. *If I Could Work.* Illustrated by Chris Winn. J. B. Lippincott, 1987.
A child considers kinds of work he would do if he were older. (Objectives 2 and 4)

Greenberg, Judith E. *What Is the Sign for Friend?* Illustrated by Gayle Rothschild. Franklin Watts, 1985.
Shane, who is hearing impaired, enjoys the friendship of other children on the playground, in the classroom, and after school. (Objectives 2 and 3)

Hutchins, Pat. *Changes, Changes.* Macmillan, 1971.
A wood block man and woman escape danger by working together. (Objective 2)

Linn, Margot. *A Trip to the Dentist.* Illustrated by Catherine Siracusa. Harper & Row, 1988.
Simple questions allow children's participation in information about a visit to the dentist's office. (Objectives 3 and 4)

——. *A Trip to the Doctor.* Illustrated by Catherine Siracusa. Harper & Row, 1988.
Simple questions invite children to be involved in information about procedures followed in a check-up. (Objectives 3 and 4)

Lionni, Leo. *Swimmy.* Pantheon, 1963.
A lonely little black fish teaches the others how to work together to scare the big fish away. (Objectives 1 and 2)

Maass, Robert. *Fire Fighters.* Scholastic, 1989.
Photographs enhance the description of the daily lives of fire fighters, including their training and services to the community. (Objectives 2, 3, and 4)

Miller, Margaret. *Whose Hat?* Greenwillow, 1988.
Color photos of hats represent types of adult groups, many of which provide services. (Objective 4)

Noble, Trinka Hakes. *The Day Jimmy's Boa Ate the Wash.* Illustrated by Steven Kellogg. Dial, 1980.
Jimmy's boa constrictor caused many problems during a class visit to a farm. (Objective 3)

Winthrop, Elizabeth. *The Best Friends Club.* Illustrated by Martha Weston. Lothrop, Lee & Shepard, 1988.
Lizzie has problems as she tries to organize an exclusive group. (Objective 1)

GROUP INTRODUCTORY ACTIVITY:

Preparation: Locate *Swimmy* by Leo Lionni. Using heavy paper, cut several stencils of small fish like the ones in Lionni's illustrations. Make a black fish using one of the stencils. Collect red construction paper and scissors. Cover the bulletin board with blue paper to create a simple underwater world; or, to make a more elaborate scene like

Lionni's, use sponges, paper doilies, and brushes to apply paint to white paper. Leave an uncluttered space in the scene for the students to create a large fish.

Focus: Point out the underwater scene and staple the small black fish to the place where the eye of the large fish will be. Say, "Here is a tiny fish swimming all alone in the ocean. Can you think of any dangers he may have to face?" Lead students to discuss the concept of big fish eating little fish.

Objective: To focus on the benefits and responsibilities of working together as a team, tell the class, "The book we are going to share is about how a little black fish thought of a way to use teamwork to make himself and his friends safe from the big, hungry fish. When I finish reading, we will discuss his idea."

Guided Activity: Read Lionni's *Swimmy*. Let the children talk about how the little fish felt before they worked together. What was Swimmy's idea? Why did it work? One of the reasons Swimmy's idea worked is that all of the red fish looked alike. Some groups of people who work as a team wear uniforms so they will look alike. Can the students think of any groups of adults or children who wear uniforms? Swimmy and his friends together made what is called a "school of fish." Encourage students to think of ways they can benefit by working together at their school.

Using the stencils and red construction paper, let each child make a fish. Put them together as Swimmy did on the bulletin board to make one big fish.

Extending Activity: Invite representatives of organizations that children can join to speak to the class. Include scouts, athletic teams, and any other group available for children in the community.

FOLLOW-UP ACTIVITIES FOR TEACHER AND STUDENTS TO SHARE:

1. Read Terence Blacker's *If I Could Work* to the class. Let the children identify the name of the group pictured on each page before the text is read. Discuss the equipment used and services performed by each. In which of the jobs are people working together as a team? Why is teamwork necessary? After completing the book, let children tell the class which job they would seek if they could work. Why? Have children talk about what they can do now to prepare for a future job.

2. Before reading Judith Greenberg's *What Is the Sign for Friend?*, let the children talk about the problems a hearing

impaired child might have in their classroom. Ask them to examine the photographs and hand signs as the text is read. After reading the book, let the children give examples of how good citizenship on the part of his classmates helped Shane. In what ways did Shane and other students work together as a team? Teach the students to sign "friend," "read," "television," "sleep," and "love." If there is a special teacher for the hearing impaired, ask him/her to talk to the class about how hearing impaired children are taught and to suggest ways all children can work and play together.

Have the students put cotton in their ears and try to function for a morning in the class. Let them discuss the problems they encountered. How could a child who could hear have helped them? Were there any benefits to not hearing all that went on?

3. Ask the group to name some things they have built with wood blocks. What has sometimes happened to the things they built? Introduce Pat Hutchins's *Changes, Changes* by telling students there are no words in the story, so they will need to help read the pictures. Ask students to notice how the two worked together to build something, what happened to the object they built, and what they built next to escape danger. After the students share the story aloud, talk about what the two did to try to escape the first problem they faced. Let students discuss why it is easier to work together on something big than to do it alone. Have children work in pairs to build something. Pretend a disaster happens to the thing they built. What could they build now to help matters?

4. While sharing Margot Linn's *A Trip to the Dentist*, let the students answer the author's questions before lifting the folded page. After reading the book, ask why the dentist is called an adult helper. What tools does the dentist use? What can children do to help the dentist care for their teeth? Contact the local health department to arrange for a dental hygienist to speak to the class about dental health and how dentists and hygienists work together. What different responsibilities does each have?

5. While sharing Margot Linn's *A Trip to the Doctor*, let the students answer the author's questions before lifting the folded page. After reading the book, have the children talk about reasons to go to the doctor. In what ways are doctors and nurses adult helpers? What can a child do at home to accept responsibility for his/her own good health? How can one child be a good school citizen in protecting the health of others in the class?

6. Read to the class *Fire Fighters* by Robert Maass. Discuss how fire fighters help citizens. Why do fire fighters work together as a team? In what ways is the job a dangerous one? Does teamwork make the job less dangerous? Why? What can a child do to help prevent fires? List student responses. Duplicate the responses on a page titled "I Can Prevent Fires By. . . ." Give a copy to each child so she or he can illustrate a border and take it home to share with the family. The teacher may want to use this book during Fire Prevention Week and arrange a field trip to a fire station.

7. Ask the students to participate in reading Margaret Miller's *Whose Hat*? Let them read the two words "Whose hat?" on each page. When they identify the hat, turn the page to see if they are right. After sharing the book, let students decide which hats belong to adult helpers and recall what each was pictured as doing? Discuss other tasks each of those helpers would perform. From a collection of helpers' hats, or pictures of hats pinned on a basic hat, select one for the group to identify. Allow a volunteer to wear the hat and pantomime a task that the represented helper might do. Ask the other students to guess the task. Continue with different hats and volunteers.

8. To introduce Trinka Hakes Noble's *The Day Jimmy's Boa Ate the Wash*, remind the students of a recent field trip or special occasion in which they participated. Discuss a behavior the group or an individual student displayed that showed good citizenship. Encourage them to listen as you read the story and think about how good school citizens should behave on a field trip. After the reading ask if they noticed any behaviors that could be called good citizenship. Were there any behaviors that could be called "bad" citizenship? Does the class think the teacher in the story will want to take her class on another field trip? Let the students vote "yes" or "no," documenting specific incidents that caused them to decide. Let the students pretend they have joined the class described in the story. Ask them to help the teacher in the story develop a list of guidelines of appropriate behavior for the next trip.

9. Before reading Elizabeth Winthrop's *The Best Friends Club* to the class, ask them if they belong to any organized groups, i.e., church, scouts, school. Give them time to discuss the values of membership in these groups. Read the story. What could have been the value of a club for best friends? What spoiled the club that Lizzie and Harold formed? If the class were to form a "Best Friends Club," what rules could they think of that would have value?

Transportation

STUDENT OBJECTIVES:

1. Identify types of transportation used by families today.
2. List the modes of transportation used in delivering goods and services.
3. Place vehicles on a timeline of historical development.
4. Decide why one form of transportation might be selected over another.
5. Identify terms associated with transportation.
6. Discuss safety concerns related to transportation.

RECOMMENDED READINGS:

Ames, Lee. *Draw 50 Vehicles.* Doubleday, 1976.
  Gives a step-by-step illustrated method for drawing land, water, and air vehicles for travel. (Objectives 1 and 3)

Barton, Byron. *Airport.* Thomas Y. Crowell, 1982.
  Illustrations and brief text show a traveler arriving at the airport, boarding the plane, and taking off. (Objectives 1 and 5)

———. *I Want to Be an Astronaut.* Thomas Y. Crowell, 1988.
  A child wishes to go on a mission to outer space. (Objectives 2 and 3)

Brown, Laurie Krasny and Brown, Marc. *Dinosaurs Travel.* Little, Brown, 1988.
  Dinosaur characters are shown using many modes of transportation as they take short and long trips. (Objectives 1, 4, 5, and 6)

Crews, Donald. *Freight Train.* Greenwillow, 1978.
  Brief text and colorful illustrations describe a steam engine pulling a variety of cars to its destination. (Objectives 2, 3, and 5)

Gibbons, Gail. *Trains.* Holiday House, 1987.
  Simple text and illustrations identify early trains and the function of a variety of present day train cars. (Objectives 2, 4, and 5)

———. *Trucks.* Thomas Y. Crowell, 1981.
  Pictures show various trucks that serve people. (Objectives 2, 4, and 5)

Hoban, Tana. *I Read Signs.* Greenwillow, 1983.
  Color photographs of signs seen along city streets. (Objective 6)

Levinson, Riki. *I Go with My Family to Grandma's.* Illustrated by Diane Goode. E. P. Dutton, 1986.
Using different modes of transportation, five families arrive at Grandma's Brooklyn home. (Objectives 3, 4, and 5)

Livingston, Myra Cohn. *Up in the Air.* Illustrated by Leonard Everett Fisher. Holiday House, 1989.
Figurative language and striking illustrations give an imaginative picture of airplane travel. (Objectives 1 and 4)

Lyon, David. *The Biggest Truck.* Lothrop, Lee, & Shepard, 1988.
Jim drives a truck all night in order to deliver strawberries to the big town. (Objective 2)

McPhail, David. *Pig Pig Rides.* E. P. Dutton, 1982.
As Pig Pig and his mother eat breakfast, they talk about the amazing things Pig Pig will do that day. (Objectives 4 and 5)

100 Words about Transportation. Illustrated by Richard Brown. Harcourt Brace Jovanovich, 1987.
Items concerning transportation are illustrated, labeled, and arranged in categories. (Objectives 1, 2, 3, 4, 5, and 6)

Scarry, Richard. *Cars and Trucks and Things That Go.* Gallaudet University Press, 1974.
The Pigs see many amazing modes of transportation as they travel to the beach for a picnic. (Objectives 1, 2, and 5)

GROUP INTRODUCTORY ACTIVITY:

Preparation: Locate *Dinosaurs Travel* by Laurie Krasny Brown and Marc Brown. Gather a globe, transparent tape, and a piece of string long enough to extend around the globe twice.

Focus: Show students the globe and tell them you are going to plan a dream trip around the world. Tape one end of the string to the class's state and say, "On my trip I will start at home and go to New York City to see the Statue of Liberty." As each new place is mentioned, tape the string to that spot on the globe. Continue, "Then I'll cross the ocean to Paris, France to climb the Eiffel Tower and down to Kenya for an African safari." The teacher may develop any itinerary she or he chooses. Only the concept of going from one place to another and finally returning to the starting point is important.

Objective: To identify types of transportation used by families today and to consider why one form of transportation might be selected over another, say, "I want you to help me decide the best ways to travel. The book I am going to read will give us some ideas. When I finish we will make a list of the kinds of vehicles to use on a trip around the world."

Guided Activity: Read aloud *Dinosaurs Travel* by Laurie and Marc Brown. Discuss rules for personal safety when traveling (pages 28 and

29). What ways can be chosen for sleeping and eating when one is traveling (pages 24–27)? Why did the family sometimes choose to ride bicycles while other times they chose to travel by train, boat, or airplane? What is a good way to cross an ocean? A desert? Mountains? Summarize student responses about selecting forms of transportation. Return to the globe and follow the string around the world, letting students list their favorite kind of vehicle to use for traveling each leg of the journey.

Extending Activity: Turn to the last page of the book and show students the picture of the young dinosaur dreaming about his next trip. Brainstorm places the students would like to go. Let them draw a picture of their favorite idea. Mount the pictures on "dream clouds" as in the book's illustration and put them on a bulletin board titled "Traveling in My Dreams."

FOLLOW-UP ACTIVITIES FOR TEACHER AND STUDENTS TO SHARE:

1. Before sharing *Draw 50 Vehicles* by Lee Ames, explain that it shows how to draw modern and old-fashioned ways to travel by land, water, and air. As each illustration is shared, ask students to identify the mode of transportation. Is it designed to be useful, recreational, or both? Was it used in the past or is it used today? After sharing the illustrations, suggest that the children use the steps Ames suggests to draw a picture of a vehicle in which they would like to ride. Display the drawings on a simple timeline in the order of their development. Leave ample space for additions to the timeline as the transportation unit progresses.

2. Read aloud Byron Barton's *Airport*. Re-examine the illustrations, letting students talk about each picture. Discuss specific terms related to flying. Visit an airport or invite a pilot to talk to the class about his/her job and training.

3. Ask the students if anyone would like to be an astronaut. Why? Why not? Ask the class to listen to Byron Barton's *I Want to Be an Astronaut* to find out what duties the child narrator would like to perform if she or he were an astronaut. After reading, let the students think about what kinds of factories might be built in space. The child in the story wants to repair a satellite. What services do satellites perform? If a class transportation timeline has been established, place the space shuttle in its appropriate sequence.

   Using the book's simple illustrations of space technology as a model, let students draw, color, and cut out their favorite item to be hung on a space mobile.

4. To introduce *Freight Train* by Donald Crews, locate a picture of a modern diesel freight train engine. Show students the picture and ask them to share a time they saw one like it. Tell them the story they will hear is about an earlier freight train engine that was powered by steam. Read the book, stopping to talk about the contents carried by each car pictured.

   After sharing the book, let students decide which kind of train car they would like to be. Have a student wanting to be the engine stand at the front of the class. As the book is read again, let students "hook on" to the engine as their car is named. As the train in the story moves, encourage students to move their "train" in a way that interprets the text imaginatively. If a transportation timeline has been developed, place the title of this book or the words "steam engine" in the appropriate place.

5. Before reading *Trains* by Gail Gibbons, duplicate the outline of various types of cars on trains. See how many the children can identify. Read the book, calling attention to the cars the students were unable to identify. What service does a freight train perform? Why might one choose to travel by passenger train rather than by car? Have the students color the train cars and make a paper train chalkboard border.

6. Share Gail Gibbons's *Trucks* with the class. Give students time to study the pictures, identifying the specific types of trucks and telling about the services they perform. Let the students illustrate their favorite truck and create a sentence about how it helps people. The teacher can copy this sentence below the picture.

7. Share each of the signs in Tana Hoban's *I Read Signs*. Talk about where one might see each of the signs. What is the use of each? Which signs relate to transportation safety in any way? Make a list of the safety signs. Suggest the students watch for safety signs for a week and report back on any they see. As new ones are reported, add them to the list.

8. Read aloud Riki Levinson's *I Go with My Family to Grandma's*. Go back and review the illustrations, asking the students to identify the means of transportation used by each family. Decide why each family chose that particular mode. Is that form of transportation still used by families today? For fun let the students select one child pictured in the book and follow him/her through the illustrations. What did that child do at Grandma's?

9. Before reading Myra Cohn Livingston's *Up in the Air,* ask students to listen carefully and use their imaginations to "see" pictures of the forests, lakes, hills, and roads. Read the poem without showing the illustrations. Do the students recall any figurative language that paints interesting pictures in their minds, e.g., "White ropes of road unwind. . . ." Read the story poem again, this time sharing the illustrations. After each page let students talk about the word pictures, using Fisher's illustrations as clues. Ask students to suppose this is a story about a family taking a trip. Why might they have chosen to fly? Where might they be going? If a family flies instead of going by car, what are the differences in the baggage they take?

10. Ask students if they have ever seen big trucks traveling on the highway. What service do these trucks do for people? Tell students *The Biggest Truck* by David Lyon shows how truck drivers deliver fresh food to people. Read the book, encouraging the class to participate in the sounds the truck makes as it travels to the town. Invite a truck driver to visit the school in his/her truck to answer the students' questions about trucks and to allow them to see inside the cab.

11. Ask students to pretend they are old enough to drive. Have them discuss the most exciting way they can imagine to travel. Tell them David McPhail's *Pig Pig Rides* is about a youngster who likes to travel in his imagination. Read the book. Have the students pantomime driving a vehicle, making the appropriate propulsion sounds. Let the class guess the mode of transportation.

12. Before sharing Richard Brown's illustrations in *100 Words about Transportation,* ask students to notice the safety devices used with the various modes of transportation. As you share each page, encourage students to participate in the reading by observing the illustrations and the first letter of the words. After sharing the book, ask students to recall any safety devices they noticed, e.g., knee and elbow pads, helmets, seat belts, flotation jackets.

   Draw two large intersecting circles on the chalkboard. Label one "Work Vehicles" and the other "Recreational Vehicles." Have students think of forms of transportation that can be classified in each category. Write the names in the appropriate circle. If any form can be classified both ways, place its name in the section where the two circles intersect. If the class has made a transportation timeline, locate vehicles in their appropriate sequence of historical development.

13. Read aloud the first few pages of Richard Scarry's *Cars and Trucks and Things That Go.* As each page is read, take time to discuss the scene and the forms of transportation presented. Point out the curious vehicles made of fruits and vegetables. After reading, let the students make carrot cars with slices of carrot for wheels. Toothpicks broken in half can hold the parts together.

For the next few weeks, allow students to take the book home for an evening to share with their families. Encourage them to seek family help in making a fanciful vehicle based on those in the illustrations. Ask students to bring their creations to school to share with the class.

Holidays

STUDENT OBJECTIVES:

1. Locate holidays on a calendar and arrange them in sequence on a timeline.
2. List symbols common to specific holidays.
3. Recognize holidays that are celebrated for individual family members.
4. Identify specific hero birthdays that have become public holidays.

RECOMMENDED READINGS:

Adler, David A. *A Picture Book of Abraham Lincoln.* Illustrated by John and Alexandra Wallner. Holiday House, 1989.
Briefly describes the life of Lincoln from a log cabin to the White House. (Objectives 2 and 4)

———. *A Picture Book of George Washington.* Illustrated by John and Alexandra Wallner. Holiday House, 1989.
Brief description of events that caused Washington to become the "Father of Our Country." (Objectives 2 and 4)

———. *A Picture Book of Martin Luther King, Jr.* Illustrated by Robert Casilla. Holiday House, 1989.
Briefly describes the contributions of the minister who worked for civil rights. (Objectives 2 and 4)

Cazet, Denys. *December 24th*. Bradbury, 1986.
Two little rabbits give a present to their grandfather after he guesses what special day it is. (Objectives 1, 2, and 3)

Gibbons, Gail. *Christmas Time*. Holiday House, 1982.
Many customs and symbols of Christmas are identified. (Objective 2)

————. *Thanksgiving Day*. Holiday House, 1983.
Describes the reason for the first Thanksgiving, how it was celebrated then, and how it is celebrated now. (Objectives 1 and 2)

Hill, Eric. *Spot's Birthday Party*. G. P. Putnam's Sons, 1982.
In this participation book, Spot finds all his hidden friends before they give him the presents they brought. (Objectives 2 and 3)

Kroll, Steven. *Happy Father's Day*. Illustrated by Marylin Hafner. Holiday House, 1988.
When Father wakes up, the family has special gifts for him to locate. (Objectives 1 and 3)

————. *Happy Mother's Day*. Illustrated by Marylin Hafner. Holiday House, 1985.
When Mother arrives home, her family has many surprises for her. (Objectives 1 and 3)

Kunhardt, Edith. *Trick or Treat, Danny!* Greenwillow, 1988.
Even though Danny is ill and cannot go trick-or-treating, others help him have fun. (Objectives 1 and 2)

Nerlove, Miriam. *Hanukkah*. Albert Whitman, 1989.
A little boy and his family prepare for the Hanukkah celebration. (Objectives 1 and 2)

Rylant, Cynthia. *Birthday Presents*. Illustrated by Sucie Stevenson. Orchard, 1987.
A child listens to a description of her birthdays beginning with the day when she was born. (Objective 3)

Spier, Peter. *Peter Spier's Christmas!* Doubleday, 1983.
This textless book illustrates the Christmas season from preparation to clean-up. (Objective 2)

Zolotow, Charlotte. *Over and Over*. Illustrated by Garth Williams. Harper & Row, 1957.
Identifies the holidays the little girl celebrates in succession from the first snow to her birthday. (Objective 1)

GROUP INTRODUCTORY ACTIVITY:

Preparation: Locate *December 24th* by Denys Cazet. The book can be used early in the school year as an introduction to the calendar and the sequence of holidays. From colored construction paper cut out enough small birthday cakes for each student and a traditional symbol to represent each of the holidays presented in the book (New Year's Day, Lincoln's Birthday, Valentine's Day, Washington's Birthday, Easter, Fourth of July, Halloween, Thanksgiving, and Christmas). The symbols can be made easily with an Ellison die press. Develop a one-year timeline divided into 12 months. The timeline should be large enough to hold the symbols and birthday cakes and placed so that it can be referred to throughout the year.

Focus: Show students a calendar and point out various holidays. Tell students a year can also be displayed on a timeline which makes it easy to tell the order in which holidays are celebrated.

Objective: In response to the objectives of locating holidays on a calendar, arranging them on a timeline, and considering holiday symbols, hold Cazet's *December 24th* for the children to see. Direct their attention to the title. Can anyone tell why December 24 is a special day? Show the date on the calendar and identify it as Christmas Eve. Ask the students to listen and find out why the rabbit family thought December 24 was an "extra special" day.

Guided Activity: After reading the story, locate on a calendar the holidays that Grandpa dressed up to represent. For each of these let the students recall the symbols he used to help the rabbit children guess. What other symbols are often used for these holidays? Locate on a calendar the holidays the rabbit children named for which Grandpa did not dress. Ask the students what symbols are used for these holidays. Let students take turns taping the prepared holiday symbols in the appropriate place on the timeline. Assist each student in writing his/her name and birth date on a small paper birthday cake. Let students put their cakes on the timeline.

Extending Activities: Throughout the year, continue to fill in the timeline with other holidays and special school events.

FOLLOW-UP ACTIVITIES FOR TEACHER AND STUDENTS TO SHARE:

1. Before reading David Adler's *A Picture Book of Abraham Lincoln*, point out February 12 on the calendar. Tell students this is the date Lincoln was born, but the national holiday is now celebrated along with Washington's birthday on President's Day. Have the class tell why they think Lincoln's birthday is recognized. List the students' responses. After reading the book, have students add to their list of reasons why his birthday is remembered. Ask if they can suggest why a log cabin and an axe are often used as symbols for Lincoln's birthday. Using Lincoln Logs, let the students build a log cabin for display.

2. Before reading David Adler's *A Picture Book of George Washington*, point out February 22 on the calendar and

have the class tell why they think Washington birthday is recognized. List the students' responses. After reading the book, have students add to their list of reasons why his birthday is remembered. Ask if they know why cherries and a hatchet are often used as symbols for Washington's birthday. Tell the class the legend of Washington's cutting down the cherry tree. Since the event never really happened, what other symbol can they suggest for his birthday?

3. Locate the third Monday in January on the calendar. Read David Adler's *A Picture Book of Martin Luther King, Jr.* What happened to Martin Luther King as a child and later to people around him that made him decide to become leader of a peaceful movement to change attitudes? Have the students ever observed unjust treatment of people because of the color of their skin?

   Because Martin Luther King Day is a new holiday for our country, no symbol has emerged for it. Have students discuss what might be a good symbol for the day. Ask the art teacher or a talented older child to design one or several of the students' ideas. Make copies for the students to keep. Choose one symbol to add to the holiday timeline.

4. Read *Christmas Time* by Gail Gibbons to the class. Have the students discuss any of the customs or symbols portrayed in the book that are also part of their family Christmas celebration. Assist small groups of students in planning and presenting a pantomime of one of the customs mentioned for the rest of the class to guess.

5. Locate this year's date for Thanksgiving on the calendar. Read Gail Gibbons's *Thanksgiving Day*. Note that the first-page sentence, "Thanksgiving is celebrated on the last Thursday of November," is not accurate for all years. Thanksgiving is celebrated on the fourth Thursday in November. Let the children discuss ways in which our celebration of Thanksgiving today reminds them of the first Thanksgiving. What are symbols we associate with Thanksgiving? Why is each one used?

   Use an overhead projector or opaque projector to enlarge a line drawing of a turkey to poster size. Let the students decorate it by glueing a variety of dried legumes and corn to the picture.

6. Before sharing Eric Hill's *Spot's Birthday Party*, talk about the games played at birthday parties. As you share the book, let the students guess the animal before lifting the page door. Talk about each clue that made a guess possible. Let the children pretend they have been invited to Spot's birth-

day party. Direct students to find or draw a picture of an appropriate gift. Using the technique from Hill's book, have them cover the picture with a flap that can be lifted, leaving a small part of the present showing. Let students take turns guessing one another's present and then lifting the flap to see if the guess was accurate. Play a party game and share cake or cookies.

7. Before reading *Happy Mother's Day* by Steven Kroll, locate the month of May on the calendar and talk about the holidays that come before and after Mother's Day. After reading the story talk about all the special gifts that were made or done at home without spending money. Was the mother happy with these gifts? Why? Let the students think of other gifts that could be made or done for a mother without spending money. Record their suggestions and save the list to compare with a future list of gifts for fathers. Add Mother's Day to the holiday timeline.

8. Because Father's Day is held at a time when many children are out of school, the teacher may want to read Steven Kroll's *Happy Father's Day* the week after Mother's Day. Before reading the book, locate Father's Day and the last day of school on the calendar. Add Father's Day and the last day of school to the holiday timeline. After reading, follow the same pattern of discussion as for *Happy Mother's Day.* Compare the list of gifts for fathers with the one the students made for mothers. Are any of the suggestions the same?

   Have students discuss their father's or a special adult's favorite sports team. Let students make construction paper pennants of the appropriate color for them to give as an "unfather's day" present.

9. Before reading Edith Kunhardt's *Trick or Treat, Danny!*, locate Halloween on the calendar. Let the children talk about what holiday comes just before and after Halloween. Read the story to the class. Have students recall all the costumes and symbols of Halloween that were a part of either text or pictures. Are there other Halloween symbols that were not included? Print "Halloween" on the chalkboard. Let the students use colored chalk to draw their favorite symbol for a border around the word.

10. Before reading Miriam Nerlove's *Hanukkah*, ask students to listen for all the things that make Hanukkah special for the children in the family. After the story is read let students recall special aspects of the holiday. Turn to the illustrations again as needed. Ask a Jewish member of the community to visit the class to discuss Hanukkah traditions and answer

students' questions. Perhaps she or he will bring a menorah and dreidel. The teacher may want to provide latkes (potato pancakes) or sufganiyah (jelly filled doughnuts) for students to share with the visitor. Have students select a symbol for Hanukkah to add to the holiday timeline.

11. Read Cynthia Rylant's *Birthday Presents* aloud. After reading the story, let students recall a favorite past birthday. Return to the book to review the child's fourth birthday. Let the students color the border of a paper plate and draw in its center the favorite birthday gift they have received.

12. During the month of December, share no more than two double spread pages of *Peter Spier's Christmas!* with the children each day. Begin with the front end-papers. Let the children study the illustrations carefully and begin a list of all the customs or symbols associated with Christmas that they can identify. Write the list on butcher paper and have the children illustrate an appropriate border as additions are made to the list each day. Encourage children to study the illustrations carefully so no details are missed. Finish the list on the last school day before Christmas vacation.

13. The teacher may want to read Charlotte Zolotow's *Over and Over* during the last month of school as a review of the holidays experienced throughout the year. After reading the book aloud, ask students what holidays were discussed in the story. As holidays are recalled, have students point to them on the timeline. Did the story mention any special occasions not on the class holiday timeline? "Summer vacation" may not have been identified. If not, write "summer vacation" across the months school will be out. What holidays will happen during the summer vacation? Ask students to talk about the colors associated with the various holidays. Using tubes of colored frosting, let the children decorate a sugar cookie in a way that reminds them of their favorite holiday.

Chapter 2
Second Grade/Third Grade

Native American Communities

STUDENT OBJECTIVES:

1. Recognize the variety of Native American communities.
2. Discuss the role of children in early Native American society.
3. Describe the household, recreational, and cultural activities of Native American communities.
4. Share the folklore of Native American communities.

RECOMMENDED READINGS:

And It Is Still That Way. Collected by Byrd Baylor. Trails West, 1988. (pa.)
Forty tribal legends are retold by Southwest Indian children. (Objective 4)

Batherman, Muriel. *Before Columbus.* Houghton Mifflin, 1981.
Introduces the homes, clothing, and daily life of the first Americans. (Objectives 1 and 3)

Baylor, Byrd. *The Desert Is Theirs.* Illustrated by Peter Parnall. Charles Scribner's Sons, 1975.
Describes how the lives of the Desert People have much in common with that of the desert animals. (Objective 1)

―――. *When Clay Sings.* Illustrated by Tom Bahti. Aladdin, 1972.
Designs in pottery are used to share the daily life of early Southwest Indian tribes. (Objectives 1, 3, and 4)

de Paola, Tomie. *The Legend of the Indian Paintbrush.* G. P. Putnam's Sons, 1988.
The origin of the state flower of Wyoming is told in the legend of a young Indian artist who served his people. (Objectives 2, 3, and 4)

Goble, Paul. *The Gift of the Sacred Dog.* Bradbury, 1980.
Presents a Plains Indian folktale about how the Great Spirit sent the horse to benefit his hungry people. (Objectives 2, 3, and 4)

Kessel, Joyce. *Squanto and the First Thanksgiving.* Illustrated by Lisa Donze. Carolrhoda, 1983.
Describes the contribution of Squanto who taught the Pilgrims how to survive the winter and raise crops. (Objectives 1 and 3)

Wheeler, M. J. *First Came the Indians.* Illustrated by James Houston. Atheneum, 1983.
Briefly describes the household and cultural life of six Indian tribes. (Objectives 1 and 3)

GROUP INTRODUCTORY ACTIVITY:

Preparation: Locate M. J. Wheeler's *First Came the Indians* and John Fandel's poem "Indians" in *Reflections on a Gift of Watermelon Pickle* (Lothrop, Lee & Shepard, 1966). Prepare a sheet of chart-sized tablet paper with the title "When Indians Are Mentioned." Write "I think of" below the title. Make a large outline map of the United States.

Focus: To introduce the Native American Communities unit, read John Fandel's poem "Indians" to the class. What does the poet think of when Indians are mentioned? As the students answer, write their responses to complete the "I think of" line on the "When Indians Are Mentioned" tablet. What do the students think of when Indians are mentioned? Allow several to add their own "I think of" lines to the tablet. Read the poem again. Ask if the students suppose the author would like to know more about Indians. Is there a line in the poem that makes them feel that way?

Objective: As a way of approaching the objectives of discussing the variety of Native American communities and of describing their household, recreational, and cultural activities, point out that Fandel used the word "wigwam" in his poem. Tell the students that some Indians of long ago used wigwams for homes, but Indians in other parts of the country lived in other kinds of houses.

Guided Activity: Tell the students that M. J. Wheeler's *First Came the Indians* introduces six North American Indian tribes. Ask them to listen for how the tribes found food, what jobs family members did, and what their homes were like. Read about the Creek, Iroquois, and Ojibwa. Let the children talk about how the tribes lived and the roles of members of the family. Show the students the introductory map in the book. Have students locate and label on the outline map where the tribes lived. The next day read about the Indians of the West. Discuss how they lived and locate the tribes on the outline map.

Extending Activity: Have the students go to the library media center as committees and find out more information and pictures about an Indian tribe of their choice. Dennis Fradin's *The Shoshoni* (Children's Press, 1988) is one of the True Book series which should be helpful for research. A number of books in the series tell about specific Indian tribes. Let the children share with the class the information they found and locate the researched tribe on the outline map.

Invite an American Indian to the class. Ask him or her to discuss the way of life of Indians today.

FOLLOW-UP ACTIVITIES FOR TEACHER AND STUDENTS TO SHARE:

1. Introduce the legends told by Indian children in *And It Is Still That Way* by sharing with students what Byrd Baylor tells in the introduction about collecting the stories. Read aloud the stories "How the Papagos Got Some Shade," "Why Navajos Live in Hogans," and "Why We Have Dogs in Hopi Villages." Discuss the meaning of any new Indian words found in the stories. How is the life of the people described in the stories like people's lives today? How is it different? After reminding students that these are family and tribal stories that the children remembered and wrote down, have the students ask their parents or grandparents to tell a story about their own childhood. Let students write the story to make a class version of *And It Is Still That Way*.

2. To introduce Muriel Batherman's *Before Columbus*, locate Utah, New Mexico, Arizona, and Colorado on the map. Tell the students they will be hearing about the earliest people to inhabit the area shown on the map. Ask the class to listen in order to learn about the way of life of those people who lived thousands of years ago. Read the book in three sections. After reading "The First People," let the class discuss what is known about the people who first lived in the area. After each of the two sections that follow are read, have the class discuss the changes in life style that occurred with the passing of time. How did researchers learn about these early Americans?

3. Before reading Byrd Baylor's *The Desert Is Theirs*, tell the children that life in the desert presents many problems. Ask

them to listen for ways the desert people learn from nature and use survival methods like those of the plants and animals. After reading the book, have the children identify the many ways people use the same methods as plants and animals in order to live in the desert.

4. After reading aloud Byrd Baylor's *When Clay Sings*, ask the students what stories the pottery caused the parents to tell. What did the students learn about the way of life of these early American communities? Why would it be exciting to find pieces of pottery made by one's ancestors? Let the students make pot shards by cutting sections from salt clay that has been rolled into sheets one fourth inch thick. Salt clay can be made by kneading equal parts of moistened flour and salt. After painting designs on a shard, have each student pretend she or he found the shard and write a paragraph about why the mother made the pot and why she chose the design.

5. Before reading Tomie de Paola's *The Legend of the Indian Paintbrush*, tell the class this is a Plains Indian legend about the origin of a wildflower called the Indian Paintbrush. After reading the book, ask the class why the flower was called a paintbrush. How did the boy in the story contribute to the life of his community? Provide each student with tan colored construction paper or a grocery bag that can be shaped into a buckskin. Have them paint a picture of a tribal event that Little Gopher might have recorded.

6. Tell the students that people all over the world have stories to explain how things important to their culture have happened. Paul Goble's *The Gift of the Sacred Dog* presents a Plains Indian folktale that explains how an Indian community received a beneficial gift from the Great Spirit. Read the book to the class. Can the students think of reasons why the Indians might have named the horse "sacred dog?" For historical background on the coming of the horse to Indian communities, read the author's note on the back of the title page. What tasks can horses do for the Indians that dogs cannot do? How did the coming of the horse benefit the community?

7. Read Joyce Kessel's *Squanto and the First Thanksgiving*. Let the class discuss how important Squanto was in the survival of the Pilgrims. What skills of the Indian people did he teach the Pilgrims?

Pioneer Communities

STUDENT OBJECTIVES:

1. Trace the movement of pioneer families settling on the frontier.
2. Discuss the role of children in the life of pioneer families.
3. Describe the household, recreational, and cultural activities of pioneer communities.
4. Share the folklore of frontier American communities.

RECOMMENDED READINGS:

Brenner, Barbara. *Wagon Wheels.* Illustrated by Don Bolognese. Harper & Row, 1978.
Based on a true story of a black pioneer family who sought the free land offered in Nicodemus, Kansas. (Objectives 1, 2, and 3)

Brown, Marc. *Party Rhymes.* E. P. Dutton, 1988.
Carefully illustrated directions and music make it easy to share the folk songs and circle games often played at parties. (Objective 3)

Coerr, Eleanor. *The Josefina Story Quilt.* Illustrated by Bruce Degen. Harper & Row, 1986.
As she rode a covered wagon West in 1850, a young girl records her experiences on quilt squares. (Objectives 1 and 2)

Gross, Ruth Belov. *If You Grew Up with George Washington.* Illustrated by Jack Kent. Scholastic, 1982.
Gives facts about the way of life of people who lived in Washington's lifetime. (Objectives 2 and 3)

Hall, Donald. *Ox-Cart Man.* Illustrated by Barbara Cooney. Viking, 1979.
Shares a nineteenth century New England farm family as the father takes their year's work to sell in the city. (Objectives 2 and 3)

Harvey, Brett. *Cassie's Journey.* Illustrated by Deborah Kogan Ray. Holiday House, 1988.
In first person, a young girl describes the problems in traveling by covered wagon from Illinois to California in the 1860s. (Objectives 1, 2, and 3)

Henry, Joanne Landers. *Log Cabin in the Woods.* Illustrated by Joyce Audy Zarins. Four Winds, 1988.
Shares the true experiences of 11-year-old Oliver Johnson as he lived with his family in 1832 in a log cabin in Indiana. (Objectives 2 and 3)

Hooks, William H. *Pioneer Cat.* Illustrated by Charles Robinson. Random House, 1988.
The cat, smuggled by a young girl in a wagon train going to Oregon, turns out to be a wise choice. (Objectives 1, 2, and 3)

Kellogg, Steven. *Paul Bunyan.* William Morrow, 1984.
Recounts incidents in the life of the legendary tall tale hero. (Objective 4)

————. *Pecos Bill.* William Morrow, 1986.
Recounts events in the life of the Texas tall tale hero. (Objective 4)

Levinson, Nancy Smiler. *Clara and the Bookwagon.* Illustrated by Carolyn Croll. Harper & Row, 1988.
Clara learns to read as the librarian in the first traveling library visits her father's farm. (Objectives 2 and 3)

McCurdy, Michael. *Hannah's Farm.* Holiday House, 1988.
Every family member accepts responsibilities on the early American Massachusetts farm. (Objectives 2 and 3)

Sanders, Scott Russell. *Aurora Means Dawn.* Illustrated by Jill Kastner. Bradbury, 1989.
After the hardship of traveling to Ohio by covered wagon, the Sheldon family finds they are the first to arrive at the new community. (Objective 1)

Turner, Ann. *Dakota Dugout.* Illustrated by Ronald Himler. Macmillian, 1985.
A pioneer wife describes early married life in a Dakota prairie sod house. (Objective 1)

GROUP INTRODUCTORY ACTIVITY:

Preparation: Locate *Aurora Means Dawn* by Scott Russell Sanders. Prepare an outline map of the United States on oak tag in a size large enough to cover a display table. Collect paints, brushes, flour, and salt to develop a raised, colored surface for the map. To make covered wagons, collect small match boxes, white construction paper, and four pennies or buttons for the wheels of each wagon.

Focus: To provide a focal point for the Pioneer Communities unit, assist the students in making a physical map of the United States. Mix equal parts of flour and salt with water to make a paste thin enough to be applied with a brush to the surface of the map. After the texture is brushed on, add more flour and salt to the mixture to make it the proper consistency for modeling mountain ranges. When the map is dry, paint it using greens and browns to indicate eleva-tion. Include the major mountains, rivers, and lakes that pioneers would have encountered going West. As the students model and paint the physical features of the map, ask them to discuss how these features might have presented problems for the pioneers.

Objective: To trace the movement of pioneer families settling on the frontier, introduce Scott Russell Sanders's *Aurora Means Dawn* by showing on the map the route pioneers probably would have traveled to go from Connecticut to Ohio. Have students suggest hardships a family might have faced on the journey. Tell the class the book begins after the Sheldon family reaches Ohio and are near their destination, a place called Aurora. Ask students to listen for the special hardship the family had to face when they found the land they had bought through an advertisement for cheap land.

Guided Activity: Read the book to the class. In what way was the Sheldon family a victim of false advertising? Have any of the students ever bought anything that disappointed them because it was not what an advertisement made it seem to be? In an atlas, find Aurora and Hudson in Ohio. Use the distance scale to determine how far Mr. Sheldon had to walk from Aurora to get help in Hudson. Label Aurora on the class map. Draw the route that the Sheldon's probably took from Connecticut to Ohio.

Let each student make a covered wagon using a small match box as the base. To make each wagon's covering, cut white construction paper into four-by-two-inch strips. Have students glue the short edges of the paper to the long edges of their boxes. Glue on pennies or buttons for wheels. Designate a wagon to represent the one belonging to the Sheldon family. Write *Aurora Means Dawn* on the wagon's cover and place it on the line from Connecticut to Ohio on the map.

Extending Activity: Continue to add place names, route lines, wagons, and appropriate symbols to the map as the books in the Pioneer Communities unit are read.

FOLLOW-UP ACTIVITIES FOR TEACHER AND STUDENTS TO SHARE:

1. Select a small committee to research the Homestead Act in the library media center. After the committee presents its findings to the class, introduce Barbara Brenner's *Wagon Wheels* by telling students that the story is based on the true experiences of a family who overcame many hardships as they came West to claim free land. After reading the story, let the class discuss the problems the Muldie family faced and how they solved them. Why did they live in a dugout even though the father was a carpenter? How did the Indians help them solve another problem? How did the neighbors in the new community help the boys when their father went on to find other land? Let groups of students develop dioramas depicting events in the pioneer life of the Muldie family.

2. Tell the children that Marc Brown's *Party Rhymes* has a number of songs that people shared at community parties many years ago. Read the titles and see if there are any that the students know. Begin with a familiar one such as "She'll be Coming Round the Mountain," letting the entire class participate. Go on to "Skip to My Lou" and "Pawpaw Patch." Let the children pick their favorites and go to a nursing home to share them. Urge the residents to join in on ones they know. Ask the residents to share other songs they remember from their childhood.

3. To introduce Eleanor Coerr's *The Josefina Story Quilt* ask the children if anyone has a quilt at home that was made by a member of the family. What special meaning does the quilt have for the family? Does it contain any patches from clothes they recognize? Does it tell a story? Let students discuss the possible reasons why people made quilts in pioneer times. Ask the class to listen as you read to find out the special reason Faith had for making a quilt. Read the book. How was Faith's quilt like a diary? What responsibilities did Faith have to accept in order to help the family? Have the students examine the illustration of the finished quilt on Faith's bed. Can they recall the events the squares represent?

    Let each student design a quilt square using one-half inch grid paper. Patterns may either be original or come from a book of quilt designs. Post the squares close enough together on the wall to look like a patchwork quilt.

4. Locate *If You Grew Up with George Washington* by Ruth Belov Gross. On each of seven large pieces of butcher paper, write the titles: Houses, Pleasures, School, Food, Clothing, Transportation and Communication, and Money and Laws. Read aloud from the book the three sections about houses. Let the students suggest facts about houses they want you to list. Divide the class into six groups and assign one of the topics to each group. Have each group read the appropriate section, list the important facts on the butcher paper, and color a frame that suggests the topic. Place the posters on the wall and have the committees share their findings with the class.

5. Read Donald Hall's *Ox-Cart Man* to the class. Let the class discuss the contributions the children made to the family's well-being. How did the community to which the father traveled benefit the family? Discuss the presents the father brought back for the family. Why were those particular items chosen?

6. To introduce Brett Harvey's *Cassie's Journey*, read the Preface and first page aloud. Let the class discuss why families left communities in the East and moved west to California in the 1860s. Was the decision a difficult one for many families? Why or why not? Suggest to the students that as you read the book aloud they should note the many hardships encountered by those in the wagon train. After reading the book, let students discuss the difficulties of the journey. On lined paper cut in the shape of a covered wagon, have each child pretend to have traveled in a wagon train and write one paragraph beginning "On my way to California by covered wagon, I was most afraid when. . . ." Let them illustrate their paragraphs and mount them on the wall in a line like a wagon train.

7. Before reading Joanne Landers Henry's *Log Cabin in the Woods* tell the class that this book records events which Howard Johnson recalled about his boyhood. His grandson published these reminiscences in a book called *A Home in the Woods* upon which Joanne Landers Henry based her story. Then read "A Note to Readers," the last page of the book. Each day read to the class about a different month described in the book. Let the students discuss the struggles, joys, and shared responsibilities of the family. After reading "September," let the children discuss how Indianapolis became a town.

   After the book is completed, suggest that small groups reread a favorite scene, think about the needed action and conversation, and play out the scene for the class.

8. Before reading *Pioneer Cat* by William H. Hooks, ask the students to pretend they are pioneer children who can take only one personal item in the family's covered wagon. What would they choose? Ask the students to share their selection with the class. Tell them the story you will read is about a young girl who must make such a choice when her family leaves their community and joins a wagon train going West. Read the book. Was Katie's choice a wise one? Why or why not? What problems did Katie's family have on the journey? Why did they have to wait in Saint Joe instead of going on alone?

9. Display a map of the United States as you read Steven Kellogg's *Paul Bunyan* to the class. After reading the book, point out on the map: Maine, the Appalachian Mountains, the St. Lawrence River, the Great Plains, Texas, Arizona, the Grand Canyon, California, the Pacific Ocean, and Alaska. As each place is identified, ask students to recall what

event in Paul's life is associated with that location. Let students refer back to the text and illustrations as necessary.

10. Introduce Steven Kellogg's *Pecos Bill* by telling the class it is a tall tale. Tall tales take ordinary events and exaggerate them in a humorous way. Ask the students to listen for exaggeration as the book is read. After the reading, make two columns on the chalkboard: one titled "Could Have Happened" and the other titled "Could Not Have Happened." Encourage students to remember events and analyze them as to whether they could have or could *not* have happened. Write each event under the appropriate title on the chalkboard.

11. Read Nancy Smiler Levinson's *Clara and the Bookwagon.* Why did Clara's father think she need not learn to read? Let the students list at least three reasons why they feel children should learn to read. How did bookwagons help people who did not live in an organized community? If your local public library has a bookmobile, arrange to have the class visit it. Before going, tell the librarian that the class has read *Clara and the Bookwagon.* The librarian may want to discuss with the class how modern bookmobiles are similar to and different from the bookwagon described in the book, and how bookmobiles are of value to people in today's communities.

12. Introduce the illustrations in Michael McCurdy's *Hannah's Farm.* Tell the class that the illustrations are wood engravings. Wood engraving designs are cut from blocks of hard, smooth end-grain wood. After cutting the pictures into the wood, McCurdy put the blocks in his printing press and made the prints. This type of illustration was used in the early 1800s, the time described in the story. Micheal McCurdy lives on Morgan Farm in Massachusetts which was used as the model for the story.

   After reading the story aloud, discuss the responsibilities Hannah accepted. What pleasures did the family share? Why did the neighbors come to help build the barn? Would that probably be the way a barn would be built today? Let students make a simple potato print of something suggested in the story. Perhaps the class can share apple cider and compare life in the early 1800s with life nearly 200 years later.

13. Read Ann Turner's *Dakota Dugout* to the class. Let the students discuss the possible reasons why the wife cried when she saw the sod house. Why did she call it Matt's cave? What were the problems of living in such a house?

What did the wife do to make it a home? What do the students suppose would be some of the differences between the woman's life as a sod housewife and the life she leads in the town where she is walking with the girl?

Rural and Small Town Living

STUDENT OBJECTIVES:

1. List the products grown on farms in various parts of the United States.
2. Analyze the varied roles of the people on a farm.
3. Discuss the changes technology has made in rural and small town living.
4. Indicate how farm life is affected by the seasons.
5. Identify ways people earn a living in rural America.
6. Identify ways people entertain themselves in rural areas.

RECOMMENDED READINGS:

Baylor, Byrd. *The Best Town in the World.* Illustrated by Ronald Himler. Charles Scribner's Sons, 1983.
Father recalls why the folks in a small town in the Texas hills and the Canyon People of the nearby farms were so special. (Objectives 3, 5, and 6)

Cooney, Barbara. *Island Boy.* Viking, 1988.
Matthais's father cleared the land on a small New England island, and Matthais's children and grandson lived there in later years. (Objectives 1, 2, 4, and 5)

Field, Rachel. *General Store.* Illustrated by Nancy Winslow Parker. Greenwillow, 1926, 1988.
A girl imagines that someday she will own a general store and sell everything from gasoline to bolts of cloth. (Objectives 3 and 5)

Hendershot, Judith. *In Coal Country.* Illustrated by Thomas B. Allen. Alfred A. Knopf, 1987.
Describes life in a small coal mining town where the author's father worked in the mines. (Objectives 5 and 6)

Johnston, Tony. *Yonder.* Illustrated by Lloyd Bloom. Dial, 1988.
Three generations live on a farm that was founded in the nineteenth century. (Objectives 3 and 4)

Kimmelman, Leslie. *Frannie's Fruits*. Illustrated by Petra Mathers. Harper & Row, 1989.
A farm family operates a fruit and vegetable stand and sells products to summer beach visitors. (Objectives 1, 2, 4, 5, and 6)

Locker, Thomas. *Family Farm*. Dial, 1988.
Shares the struggles of a family to keep their farm and home. (Objectives 1, 2, and 5)

Provensen, Alice and Provensen, Martin. *Shaker Lane*. Viking, 1987.
A reservoir will cause Shaker Lane to be flooded and the poor residents leave rather than fight to keep their property. (Objectives 3 and 5)

Rogow, Zack. *Oranges*. Illustrated by Mary Szilagyi. Orchard, 1988.
Illustrations aid in presenting the many people involved in bringing oranges from the grove to the table. (Objectives 1, 2, 3, and 5)

GROUP INTRODUCTORY ACTIVITY:

Preparation: Locate *Oranges* by Zack Rogow and an encyclopedia article about oranges. Prepare an outline map of the United States for each student. Arrange for the students to have access to encyclopedias or other sources that provide United States farm product information in simple graph or map form. Provide oranges for the students to eat.

Focus: Give each student an outline map of the United States and ask which states they think grow the most oranges. Read the part of an encyclopedia article that tells where oranges are grown in the United States. Show the graph or map that gives production information and explain how to interpret it. Have students draw a small orange in the southern part of the states mentioned. Guide them in preparing a legend for the map that gives the meaning of the orange symbol. Discuss why oranges are grown only in warm areas.

Objective: In assisting to identify products grown on farms in the United States, in analyzing varied farm roles, and in noting the changes technology has brought, share Zack Rogow's *Oranges* with the class. Before reading the book, hold up an orange and tell the students that people work at many different jobs so that we can have oranges to eat. Ask them to listen while you read to find out what jobs people do so that we can buy oranges at the market.

Guided Activity: Read the book and then ask students to recall the jobs involved in growing and delivering oranges. As they respond, list their answers on the chalkboard. What ethnic groups were depicted? What changes in farm machinery were evident in the orange field from the time of planting to the time the field fully matured? Refer back to the book's illustrations as necessary.

Tell the students that farms in the United States produce many items besides oranges. Using an overhead projector, list some of the most important ones. You may want to include wheat, corn, apples, grapefruit, cotton, beef, milk, eggs, potatoes, peanuts, grapes, and any products important to your area. Let students work in pairs, selecting a favorite product and looking it up in an encyclopedia or other media center source. Have each pair design a symbol for their product, draw it on the outline map in the states where the item is produced, and add it to the legend. Have a small group of students combine the individual maps into one class map with a legend entry for each product. Let the rest of the class cut pictures of farm life out of magazines. Arrange the map and pictures on a bulletin board titled "Farming in the United States."

To celebrate the day's work give each student an orange. As the students eat, encourage them to remember all the hard work that was involved in getting the orange into their hands. Have students save any seeds they find.

Extending Activity: Let students plant orange seeds to make a classroom farm. The shiny, dark green leaves of the orange plant make an attractive house plant for the students to take home. Students may also want to expand their classroom farm by planting seeds or cuttings of the plants they have researched.

FOLLOW-UP ACTIVITIES FOR TEACHER AND STUDENTS TO SHARE:

1. To introduce Byrd Baylor's *The Best Town in the World*, explain that the author wrote the book for her family in order to record stories her father had told her about the special little town in Texas where he grew up. Locate Texas on a map and tape a first prize blue ribbon on the state. After reading the book, ask the class to recall the reasons why the boy thought the town was special. What did the people in the town do for recreation? How does the store compare to stores today?

   Ask the children to think about their own town or city. Would they call it the best in the world? Why or why not? Have a student who thinks his hometown is best tape a blue ribbon to the state on the map. Ask the students to interview their fathers or mothers to find out what town they think is the best in the world. Let the students report their findings to the class and tape a blue ribbon to the state of each town mentioned.

2. On a map show students the coastline of New England. Have them brainstorm ways families who live on islands along the coast might earn a living. Tell the class to listen as you read Barbara Cooney's *Island Boy* for the way the Tibbetts family made a living over three generations. After

reading the story, discuss how Matthais's father and his sons made a living. When Matthais's daughter and grandson came to live on the island, how did they earn a living? What foods were available to the Tibbits family on their island? As the students respond, record their answers using an overhead projector. After the list is made, ask students to classify each item as cultivated or naturally occurring.

3. Before reading Rachel Field's *General Store* tell the class they might hear several unfamiliar words in this poem written in 1926. Ask the students to listen to the text and look at Parker's illustrations to see if they can determine the meaning of unfamiliar words. After reading the book, ask students which words were new to them. If they fail to mention "calico," "crockery," and "sarsaparilla," discuss the meaning of those words. Read the note about sarsaparilla on the back of the Title Page. Show the illustration of the cash register. How is it different from ones used today? In what other ways is this store different from the ones the students usually go to? Read the book again so students can identify more differences. How might a general store benefit people who live in rural areas?

4. Read Judith Hendershot's *In Coal Country* to the class. Have the students tell how life at that time and place was different from their own now. What did the children do to have fun? Appoint three committees to go to the library media center for research. Have one committee locate Neffs, Ohio, on a map and report to the class what states they would go through to get from their state to Ohio. If the class is in Ohio, what roads would they take to get to Neffs? Have the second committee find the population of Neffs, Ohio, and have the third committee research what five states mine the most coal.

5. Introduce Tony Johnston's *Yonder* by telling the class that this story begins a hundred years ago. Ask the children to share in reading the book by repeating the chorus, "There. Just over there. . ." when you point to them. Ask them also to notice what early farm life was like. How was it different from today? After the book is read, ask the students to talk about the changes in farm life over the years. Look at the illustrations again. What were some things that happened at specific seasons? Particularly note the changes in the plum tree in the front yard during the different seasons. Let the children experiment with watercolors by painting a tree in their favorite season.

6. To prepare students to hear *Frannie's Fruits* by Leslie Kimmelman, ask if anyone has ever stopped at a roadside

stand to buy fruits and vegetables. What did they buy? Why did they stop at a roadside stand instead of buying these items in a grocery store? Tell the class that this is the story of a family who sold fruits and vegetables to the people who visited their area in the summer. Ask the students to look for fruits and vegetables that were sold but probably not grown on the farm. After reading the story, let the class list items the family sold. What food items were probably not grown on the farm? Why? Ask the class to suggest reasons why the fruit stand was open only in the summer. What do the students suppose the family does in the winter? What was special about this fruit stand that would make customers want to return?

Give each student a potato. Ask them to look at the potato and suggest ways to make a potato head doll like the ones Frannie urged her customers to make. Encourage students to bring items from home to add to the potato to make an original character.

7. Appoint a committee to go to the library media center and find out why the organization Farm Aid was formed. After the committee reports to the class, tell students that Thomas Locker, the author of *Family Farm*, used to live in the "Heartland of America" and is donating some of the money made from the book to Farm Aid. Read the story to the class. What problem did the farm family face? When the father got a job in town, what extra chores did the mother, grandfather, and the two children assume? What school activities did the two children give up to help the family? Why was their school closed? What farm products did the family raise at first? What crops did they start growing to help save their farm? Why did the family want to remain on the farm? Many farmers in the United States are losing their farms. Can the students think of possible reasons why this is a problem for the entire nation?

As a class, write a letter to your congressman in Washington telling him that you read a book about the difficulties of farmers. Ask what his or her position is concerning legislation to help farmers. Individual students may want to write Farm Aid asking for information about the organization. The address is: Farm Aid, 21 Erie Street, Number 20, Cambridge, Massachusetts 02139.

8. Before reading Alice and Martin Provensen's *Shaker Lane*, introduce the phrase "eminent domain" and explain its meaning. Tell students the concept is important to the story. Read the book. Why were the people in other parts of town unhappy with the residents of Shaker Lane? What things did

Big Jake Van der Loon do to earn a living and help his neighbors? Why did the land agent have the right to tell the people to leave? What is the difference between the way of life of the new families on Reservoir Road and the families on Shaker Lane? What did Old Man Van Sloop do to earn a living after the reservoir was filled? Where do the students suppose he might have obtained the antiques to start his business?

Urban Living

STUDENT OBJECTIVES:

1. Identify buildings and services associated with urban living.
2. Discuss the impact of technology on city life.
3. Compare small town and big city living.
4. Identify specific buildings and services associated with New York City.

RECOMMENDED READINGS:

Alexander, Martha. *How My Library Grew, by Dinah.* Wilson, 1983.
  Dinah records in pictures her observations of the construction of the new library and presents it as a gift to the librarian. (Objective 1)

Arnold, Caroline. *Pets without Homes.* Illustrated by Richard Hewett. Clarion, 1983.
  Photographs and text demonstrate the community service of the animal shelter. (Objective 1)

Burton, Virginia Lee. *The Little House.* Houghton Mifflin, 1942.
  The city grows up around the little house. (Objectives 2 and 3)

Carrick, Carol. *Left Behind.* Illustrated by Donald Carrick. Houghton Mifflin, 1988.
  Christopher loses his partner and is left behind on a field trip to the aquarium. (Objectives 1 and 3)

Gibbons, Gail. *The Post Office Book.* Thomas Y. Crowell, 1982.
  Shows how mail service has changed since the early days and describes modern methods of mail service. (Objective 1)

Horwitz, Joshua. *Night Markets.* Thomas Y. Crowell, 1984.
  Photographs and text explore the process of supplying New York City's people with the quantities of food they require. (Objectives 1, 2, and 4)

Isadora, Rachel. *City Seen from A to Z.* Greenwillow, 1983.
Urban living is pictured and identified by words arranged in alphabetical order. (Objectives 1 and 3)

Maestro, Betsy. *Taxi: A Book of City Words.* Illustrated by Giulio Maestro. Clarion, 1989.
As the reader follows the illustrations of a taxi driver's busy day, many terms are introduced in the brief text. (Objectives 1 and 2)

Munro, Roxie. *The Inside-Outside Book of New York City.* Dodd, Mead, 1985.
Shares special places in New York City of interest to visitors. (Objective 4)

Stevens, Carla. *Anna, Grandpa, and the Big Storm.* Illustrated by Margot Tomes. Clarion, 1982.
During New York's Great Blizzard of 1888 Grandpa and Anna are stranded on the Third Avenue El until rescued by firemen. (Objectives 1, 2, and 4)

GROUP INTRODUCTORY ACTIVITY:

Preparation: Locate *The Inside-Outside Book of New York City* by Roxie Munro. Ask a travel agent to agree to receive a phone call from the class to discuss making arrangements to travel to New York City. If possible, arrange to have access to a speaker phone in a location that allows the whole class to participate in the conversation. Collect paper, colored markers, etc., for making posters.

Focus: Tell the children that today the class is going to travel "by book" to one of America's most famous cities. Locate New York City on the map. Ask students to suggest ways one might travel from their community to New York City. Call the travel agent and ask about means of transportation to New York City, the names of airports and railway stations, lodging, and prices.

Objective: In response to the objective of identifying specific buildings and services associated with New York City, ask the children to listen as you read Roxie Munro's *Inside-Outside Book of New York City* in order to decide which place in the city they would like most to visit.

Guided Activity: Share each picture and tell students facts that will interest them from the descriptions at the end of the book. Let each student identify what she or he found most interesting about New York City and tell why the choice was made. Let students go to the library media center to find other places to visit in New York City and activities that would be fun to do there.

Tell students that agencies in big cities like New York encourage tourists to travel there. Using what they found in the book and in the library, let each student select a point of interest and make a travel poster encouraging tourists to visit that site. Ask the library media specialist to display the posters in the library along with books about New York City.

Extending Activity: Encourage students to ask their parents' permission to look through their families' record and tape collections to see if they can find any songs about New York City. If parents will allow the recordings to be brought to school, play them for the class.

FOLLOW-UP ACTIVITIES FOR TEACHER AND STUDENTS TO SHARE:

1. Read Martha Alexander's *How My Library Grew, by Dinah* to the class. Using the pictures and text as a guide, record the steps Dinah observed in the library's construction. For each step also record the workmen required and the contribution they made. Appoint two students to go to the library media center and see if they can find a book that will answer Dinah's questions about moles and rainbows. Ask them to report the answers and whether they needed help from the library media specialist. In what way did they receive assistance?

2. Read aloud Caroline Arnold's *Pets without Homes*. Ask the class to list three reasons officers pick up stray animals. Have students make a "wanted poster," describing and illustrating the dog or cat they would like to adopt. Invite an animal control officer to the class to talk about why their work is important to the community.

3. Before reading Virginia Lee Burton's *The Little House* have students look up the word "technology" in the dictionary and discuss its meaning. Show the class the end papers of the book and ask them to identify the changes in technology pictured there. List their responses on the chalkboard. Ask students to look for other evidence of technology as you read the book aloud. After reading the book, ask them how technology affected the little house. Add their responses to the list. What happened to the little house at the end of the book? What do the students think the future of the little house is? Why?

4. Ask students to tell about a favorite school field trip they have taken. What safety rules did the teacher make for the trip? Introduce Carol and Donald Carrick's *Left Behind* as a story about a boy who went on a field trip in a big city and forgot the rules. Read the book. Who finally helped Christopher find his teacher? How is a field trip in a city different from one in a small town? Why would it be more

frightening for Christopher to get lost in a large city than it would have been if he had lived in a small town?

5. Read aloud *The Post Office Book* by Gail Gibbons. Give the children time to examine the illustrations which depict the history of mail delivery. Let them locate the zip code on the map that identifies the area closest to where they live. Have students discuss where each of the illustrated mailboxes are. Are there any mailboxes located near the school or the students' homes? Designate several students to take photographs of mailboxes in the neighborhood. Plan a class visit to the local post office. Photograph the steps in processing the mail. Let students write letters to one another. Take snapshots of the writing, sending, and receiving. Use all the photographs to develop an illustrated timeline titled "Letters: How They Get from Here to There."

6. Introduce Joshua Horwitz's *Night Markets* by asking the class what modes of transportation might be used to bring food to New York City's people. Where do they think the food might come from? Read the brief text on pages 7–19. Ask the children to recall the modes of transportation mentioned. Were there some the class did not suggest before sharing the book? On a map of the world let children identify countries or regions of the United States that supply food to New York City. Have the children locate those places on the map and attach a length of yarn to a pin located at that point. Place the other end of the yarn on New York City.

   Ask for volunteers to read each of the sections: Gansevoort Meat Market (pp 20–33), Terminal Market at Hunt's Point (pp 34–41), East 14th Street (pp 42–51), the wholesale flower district of midtown Manhattan (pp 52–59), and Fulton Fish Market (pp 60–73). Have students share with the class what food products are handled at each place and locate on the map the source of the food.

7. Go through Rachel Isadora's *City Seen from A to Z* with the class. Ask the students to examine the illustrations on each page and decide whether the picture could be identified only with city living or if it could also be identified with rural living. Encourage them to justify their answers with specific examples. Ask the class to suppose they were making a city alphabet book. What activities, buildings, events, people, etc., would *they* include for each letter? Let children select a letter to illustrate. Have them write the appropriate term below their pictures. Bind the illustrations into a class "City ABC Book."

8. Before introducing *Taxi: A Book of City Words* by Betsy Maestro to the class, list on the chalkboard all the highlighted terms in the brief text. There is one such term on each page. Read the first two pages aloud. Let the students discuss how they know the illustration is of a city. Is any technology that affects city life seen in the first page's illustration? How can the students recognize that this is a city taxi and not one that serves people in a small town? Ask students to select a term from the chalkboard and read that page aloud to the class. Have each reader share the illustration, point out any city services pictured, and identify technology that affects city life. After all have shared, ask the class to recall any new words they had not heard before.

9. Before reading Carla Stevens's *Anna, Grandpa, and the Big Storm*, tell the class this story takes place during the New York blizzard of 1888. After hearing the story they will discuss any differences they see between New York 100 years ago and now. Read the book. Let the class discuss the changes technology has made in city living. If they fail to mention them, point out the gas street lamps, coal burning stoves, horse drawn fire engine, and the elevated train powered by steam. Anna did not know if school would be closed because of the storm. How do today's students find out about school closings? Who helped the people get down from the train? Do firemen still help people in trouble? In what ways?

   Ask the class to imagine a story that might happen if New York City had a great blizzard in the 1990s. Record the events they suggest and have them select a scene to illustrate.

Being an American

STUDENT OBJECTIVES:

1. Discuss what responsible citizens do for their country.
2. Identify historical buildings and monuments in Washington D.C.
3. Recognize contributions of famous Americans.

4. Describe why specific symbols are valued by United States citizens.
5. Specify examples of America's cultural diversity.

RECOMMENDED READINGS:

Aliki. *The Many Lives of Benjamin Franklin.* Simon & Schuster, 1977, 1988.
Includes Franklin's early life, his many inventions, and his contributions to his country. (Objectives 1 and 3)

————. *A Weed Is a Flower: The Life of George Washington Carver.* Simon & Schuster, 1965, 1988.
Illustrations aid the brief text in the presentation of Dr. Carver's life, focusing on his research and teaching. (Objectives 1, 3, and 5)

Coerr, Eleanor. *Chang's Paper Pony.* Illustrated by Deborah Kogan Ray. Harper & Row, 1988.
Living in San Francisco during the gold rush days, a Chinese immigrant boy finds a way to get the pony he wants. (Objectives 1 and 5)

Maestro, Betsy and Maestro, Giulio. *The Story of the Statue of Liberty.* Lothrop, Lee & Shepard, 1986.
Describes how France gave the United States the statue that became a symbol of liberty. (Objective 4)

Munro, Roxie. *The Inside-Outside Book of Washington D.C.* E.P. Dutton, 1987.
Pictures the activities within important buildings in Washington D. C., giving a brief description of each at the close of the book. (Objective 2)

Quackenbush, Robert. *Quit Pulling My Leg! A Story of Davy Crockett.* Simon & Schuster, 1987.
This biography distinguishes between the facts and legends in the life of the American frontiersman. (Objectives 1 and 3)

Sandin, Joan. *The Long Way to a New Land.* Harper & Row, 1981.
An easy-to-read account of a Swedish family who came to America in 1868. (Objectives 1 and 5)

————. *The Long Way Westward.* Harper & Row, 1989.
Relates in an easy-to-read format the journey of a Swedish immigrant family from New York to their new home in Minnesota. (Objective 5)

Spier, Peter. *The Star-Spangled Banner.* Doubleday, 1973.
With the words of the national anthem as a text, the illustrations trace United States history from the War of 1812 to the present. (Objectives 2, 3, and 4)

Stanek, Muriel. *I Speak English for My Mom.* Illustrated by Judith Friedman. Albert Whitman, 1989.
Lupe must speak English for her mother until Mrs. Gomez decides that learning English will help her get a better job. (Objective 5)

Yarbrough, Camille. *Cornrows*. Illustrated by Carole Byard. Cow-
ard-McCann, 1979.
Describes the traditional African hair designs that continue to be used by
African-Americans. (Objective 5)

GROUP INTRODUCTORY ACTIVITY:

Preparation: Locate *The Star-Spangled Banner* by Peter Spier. Ask the
music teacher to help you find a recording of the song "The Star-
Spangled Banner." Collect enough paper, red makers, and blue markers for the students to draw flags.

Focus: Before playing a recording of the national anthem, tell the
class to listen to see if they recognize the song. After playing the song,
ask if any students know its name. Do they know any of the words?
On what occasions have they heard it played? To what do the words
"star-spangled banner" refer? From the notes at the back of the book,
tell students the circumstances of Francis Scott Key's writing the
words in 1814.

Objective: In order to recognize contributions of famous Americans
and note specific symbols valued by citizens, tell the students that
Peter Spier included illustrations from the Battle of Baltimore in
1814 and illustrations of modern American scenes in his book *The
Star-Spangled Banner*. Ask them to notice the many places the American flag is displayed as you read the book.

Guided Activity: Share the book with the class, letting students join in
when they know the words. Ask students to recall the places the flag
is displayed. List their responses on the chalkboard. Go back through
the book and discuss the American landmarks and historical buildings
illustrated. Are there any that the students recognize as being in
Washington D. C.?
 Show students the endpapers in the front of the book and discuss
the variety of flags the United States has had over the years. Call students' attention to the fact that a new star is added each time a new
state joins the union. Find the flag that flew over Fort McHenry
when Francis Scott Key wrote "The Star-Spangled Banner" and the
one that was used when the students' state became part of the United
States. Let each student select a flag to draw. Display the flags on a
"Star-Spangled Banner" timeline.

Extending Activity: Select a committee of students to go to the media
center and find instructions for displaying and folding the flag for
storage. Ask the principal if the class can hoist and take down the
school's flag for a week.

FOLLOW-UP ACTIVITIES FOR TEACHER AND STUDENTS TO SHARE:

1. Before reading Aliki's *The Many Lives of Benjamin Franklin*, ask the class if they know of anything Benjamin Franklin invented or anything he did to help his country. Title two pieces of butcher paper "Inventions and Discoveries" and "How He Helped His Country in War and Peace." Tell the class to listen as you read the biography for items that can be listed under each heading. After the book is read, have students suggest facts for each list. Ask them to reread the book as they find time and add to either list.

   Ask a small group of students to review the sayings from *Poor Richard's Almanak* that are included in the book. Let them go to the library media center and try to locate more sayings by Benjamin Franklin. Have them write down and illustrate interesting ones they find.

2. Introduce Aliki's *A Weed Is a Flower: The Life of George Wshington Carver* by asking the class what they think the title means. Tell them as they listen to the book they will find the answer to your question. Read the book. What problems did George Washington Carver face as a child? In what ways did he help other people? For what things is he most remembered? Discuss things that are made from peanuts and sweet potatoes. Let the children shell and eat roasted peanuts in honor of George Washington Carver. Have them save the shells for an art project of making peanut people by gluing the shells on paper. Students may also want to grow a sweet potato plant by submerging half a sweet potato in a small vase of water.

3. Select a small group of students to read Eleanor Coerr's *Chang's Paper Pony*. Tell them this is the story of a lonely Chinese boy who lived in San Francisco during the gold rush days of the 1850s. On a map point out China and San Francisco. Discuss how people in that time would have traveled from one continent to another. Read the first three pages. Let the children suggest the meaning of the word immigrant and the problems being an immigrant caused Chang.

   Let students take turns reading the book aloud to the small group. When the book is finished, let the children hold a book discussion. What were Chang's character traits? How did he solve his problem? Does the group feel the horse will make him more acceptable to the people of San Francisco? Why or why not? Conclude the discussion by reading the author's note. If immigrants contributed to this country, why were they treated cruelly by some people? Is this the way responsible citizens behave? Ask a member of the group to volunteer to give a booktalk to encourage the rest of the class to read the book.

4. Introduce Betsy and Giulio Maestro's *The Story of the Statue of Liberty* by telling the class that the statue is a symbol of freedom in the New World. Ask them to listen for the reason she holds a lamp in her raised hand and for facts about the statue. After the book is read, list the facts they recall on butcher paper. Refer to the book to verify facts as needed. Let the class make a "fireworks" border to the list to remind them of the celebration in New York Harbor each Fourth of July.

5. Before sharing the illustrations in Roxie Munro's *the Inside-Outside Book of Washington D. C.*, locate Washington D. C. on the map. Share each picture and tell the students facts that would interest them from the descriptions at the end of the book. Go back through the book. See if the students can recall the building and any facts about it. Let individual students select a favorite Washington D. C. building to research in the library media center. Allow time for them to share their findings with the class.

6. Before reading Robert Quackenbush's biography of Davy Crockett, ask the class to share anything they already know about Davy Crockett. Where did they learn about him? Were the ideas they shared true, or just tall tales? Tell the class you are going to read a true story of Davy Crockett. Read *Quit Pulling My Leg! A Story of Davy Crockett.* You may want to take several days to read the book. After reading the biography, have the children identify the character traits of Davy Crockett that helped him serve his country. Discuss what he did because of each trait. Why do the students think tall tales were told about him?

Leave the book in the classroom so the students can read the tall tale ideas told by the little animals at the bottom of each page of text. Ask them to draw the two little animals and make a cartoon of a true fact about Davy Crockett's life.

7. Select a small group of students to read Joan Sandin's *The Long Way to a New Land*. Introduce the story to the group by reading the author's note on the last page of the book. Locate Sweden and the United States on a map. Ask a student volunteer to trace the route one would take in traveling from Sweden to the United States. Then let the small group read the story. In a book discussion setting, let

them discuss why the family came to America, the problems they faced as they left Sweden, and the difficulties of the journey. Does the group think the family will become responsible citizens of the United States? What character traits do they have that will help them succeed?

8. After a small group has read and discussed Joan Sandin's *The Long Way to a New Land*, have one student volunteer to read and report on its sequel *The Long Way Westward*. Encourage the student to show the map at the front of the book as she or he tells of the family's trip to Minnesota.

9. Read Muriel Stanek's *I Speak English for My Mom*. How will learning English be helpful to Lupe's mother? Ask the class what they think are the 10 most important English words she will need to know. Do the students think these words will be easy for her to learn? Ask a Spanish speaking resource person or use a translating dictionary to find the Spanish word for each of the 10 English words. Have the students work in small groups to learn the Spanish words. Now how hard do they think it would be for a Spanish speaker to learn 10 English words?

10. Before reading Camille Yarbrough's *Cornrows*, see if any of the children know where their great-great grandparents came from. Do they have some special traditions that their family has carried down for generations? Read the book to the class. Why did the children choose those special people for their hair name game? Why do the students think it is important to keep up family traditions? Have them ask their parents if they have any family traditions or stories that have been handed down. Let them share those stories in class.

World Neighbors

STUDENT OBJECTIVES:

1. Name and locate on a map the students' home country and continent, other countries and continents, and the oceans.
2. Show how land regions of the world affect the way people live.

3. Describe the economic and social conditions of people in specific countries of each continent as a basis for understanding world neighbors.
4. Identify art, music, dance, folklore, food, customs, and ways of life unique to various countries of the world.

RECOMMENDED READINGS:

Ancona, George. *Bananas: From Manolo to Margie.* Houghton Mifflin, 1982.
Describes life on a Honduras banana plantation and the preparation needed to export bananas to the United States. (Objectives 1, 2, 3, and 4)

Andrews, Jan. *Very Last First Time.* Illustrated by Ian Wallace. Atheneum, 1985.
Eva Padlyat, who lived in an Inuit village in northern Canada, hunts mussels alone on the bottom of the sea. (Objectives 1, 2, 3, and 4)

Balit, Christina. *An Arabian Home.* Hampstead, 1988.
An urban family visits their Bedouin relatives to celebrate a wedding. (Objectives 1, 2, 3, and 4)

Bayer, Jane. *A My Name Is Alice.* Illustrated by Steven Kellogg. E. P. Dutton, 1984.
Letters of the alphabet introduce animals around the world and their humorous activities. (Objective 1)

Baylor, Byrd. *The Way to Start a Day.* Illustrated by Peter Parnall. Charles Scribner's Sons, 1978.
Poetic text gives examples of how people around the world have celebrated the dawn. (Objectives 1 and 4)

Greenfield, Eloise. *Under the Sunday Tree.* Illustrated by Amos Ferguson. Harper & Row, 1988.
Poetry and paintings give a picture of life in the Bahamas. (Objectives 1, 2, 3, and 4)

Haskins, Jim. *Count Your Way through Russia.* Illustrated by Vera Mednikov. Carolrhoda, 1987.
Using the Russian words for numbers one through 10, concepts about Russian culture are presented. (Objectives 1, 2, and 4)

Hort, Lenny. *The Boy Who Held Back the Sea.* Illustrated by Thomas Locker. Dial, 1988.
A Dutch grandmother gives her version of the leak in the dike story. (Objectives 1 and 4)

Levinson, Riki. *Our Home Is the Sea.* Illustrated by Dennis Luzak. E.P. Dutton, 1988.
A Chinese boy lives with his family in a houseboat in Hong Kong harbor. (Objectives 1, 2, 3, and 4)

Morris, Ann. *Bread Bread Bread.* Illustrated by Ken Heyman. Lothrop, Lee & Shepard, 1989.
Describes the many kinds of bread baked around the world, identifying the country and a bit about the way of life. (Objectives 1 and 4)

————. *Hats Hats Hats*. Illustrated by Ken Heyman. Lothrop, Lee & Shepard, 1989.
Introduces purposes for wearing hats and identifies hats from a variety of countries. (Objectives 1 and 4)

Plotkin, Gregory and Rita. *Cooking the Russian Way*. Illustrated by Robert L. and Diane Wolfe. Lerner, 1986.
Shares Russian culture, food habits, and recipes. (Objective 4)

GROUP INTRODUCTORY ACTIVITY:

Preparation: Locate *Bread Bread Bread* by Ann Morris. From the list at the back of the book prepare index cards, each with the name of a different country. If the students are not proficient at identifying the names of the continents and oceans on a world map, prepare and present a lesson to review these concepts.

Focus: Tell the class they are going to hear a book that discusses one thing that many places around the world have in common. Distribute the cards among the students and let them practice saying the name of the country. Have them find the country on a map and write the name of the continent and nearest ocean on the back of the card. Tell them they will share their findings with the class after the book is read.

Objective: To address the objective of identifying food and customs unique to various countries of the world, show the students Ann Morris's *Bread Bread Bread*, and tell them that bread is the one thing each of the countries has in common. Ask them to observe the photographs and see if they can identify pictures from the country written on their cards.

Guided Activity: Read the book aloud. After reading the book, go back through the illustrations. For each photograph share the information given by the author at the back of the book. As a new country is mentioned, let the student who has a card of that place show the country on the map and identify its continent and nearest ocean.

Plan a field trip to a local bakery. Ask the baker to show the students the American breads and any breads she or he makes which are characteristic of other countries.

Extending Activity: Ask students if anybody in their families bakes bread. Do they make any of the unusual breads shown in the book? Contact those parents and arrange for them to demonstrate to the class how they make the special bread.

FOLLOW-UP ACTIVITIES FOR TEACHER AND STUDENTS TO SHARE:

1. Before reading George Ancona's *Bananas: From Manolo to Margie*, locate Honduras on a world map. Identify it as being in a tropical region. Have a student look up and read the definition of the word "tropical." See if the students can name foods that grow in tropical places. Tell the class the book will describe life on a banana plantation and the way bananas are transported to the United States. Read the book to the class. Stop reading as the bananas are loaded on the ship. What modes of transportation were used to bring the bananas from the plantation to the United States? How did the tropical climate affect the way Manolo's home was built, the family's food, and their way of life?

2. Talk to the children about tides. Tell the class that the young girl in the story is going to walk on the bottom of the ocean. What might that mean? Read Jan Andrews's *Very Last First Time* aloud. How did the people in Ungava Bay use the mussels? Look again at the book's illustrations and let the students identify how the climate affected the way people in the village lived. Locate Ungava Bay on a map. How would someone from the lower United States travel to the village? Why do the students suppose the book was given the title *Very Last First Time?* Ask the students to write a paragraph about something they did that they remember especially as the "very last first time."

3. Read Christina Balit's *An Arabian Home* to the class. Locate Arabia on a map. Discuss the difference in the way of life of Leila and Mustapha in the city and that of their Bedouin cousins. How does the desert affect the way the Bedouins live? Make a web of the concepts the students learned from *An Arabian Home*. In the center circle of the web, put the word "Bedouins." In circles extending from the center put the words "food," "social customs," "homes," "clothing," and "transportation." Let students recall details from the story and write the details in circles extending from the proper categories.

4. Before reading Jane Bayer's *A My Name Is Alice*, tell the class the verses in the book are based on an old jump rope chant they may want to learn and include in their recess activities. After reading the book, let each student choose a letter of the alphabet and select a city, state, country, or continent to use in writing a new version of *A My Name Is Alice*. Have them locate their chosen places on a map. Let

the class go outside and take turns reciting their rhymes while jumping rope.

5. Before reading Byrd Baylor's *The Way to Start a Day*, ask the class to suppose that someone has asked them how they start their day. What would they answer? After several children have responded, tell them in some parts of the world people go out and greet the sun as a way to start the day. Ask the class to notice the countries that are mentioned as you read the story. After sharing the book, see what countries they can recall. Read the story again. This time locate on a world map each country or state as it is mentioned. After this second reading, let the students discuss ways people around the world welcome the sun.

   Suggest to the students that the class write a poem to welcome the sun. Have the children share ideas of why they are glad to see the sun come up. Record their responses as an unrhymed poem. Begin and end with, "Welcome, Sun." Ask someone to practice reading the poem. The next morning that the sun is shining, go outside as a class and welcome the sun. Let the entire class say the opening and closing lines while the one student reads the other part of the poem.

6. Locate the Bahamas on the map and tell the class that Eloise Greenfield's poetry and Amos Ferguson's paintings in *Under the Sunday Tree* will give them an idea of life there. Read the poem "Traditions." Talk about whether carrying things on your head would be easy. What does the last line, "We also carry history," mean? Read "Thoughts." Tell the class that in the Bahamas the policeman stands in the middle of the street and directs traffic. What controls the traffic flow in our cities? Read "When the Tourists Come to Town." How do the tourists appear to those who live in the Bahamas? Why do tourists go there? Ask the children if they have ever ridden in a horse drawn carriage down city streets. Read "To Catch a Fish" and "The Sailboat Race." Look at the map again. Why do the students suppose those are popular sports in the Bahamas?

7. Before reading *Count Your Way through Russia* by Jim Haskins, locate the Soviet Union on the globe. Can the students make a prediction about the climate of this country located near the North Pole? Tell the class that both Russia and the Soviet Union are names that are commonly used and that Russia is actually one large area within the Soviet Union. Ask them to share anything they know about the Russian way of life. While reading the book, encourage students to repeat the words for numbers. Have the students

share any new information they learned about Russia and its people. What are some similarities between Russia and the United States? Have students divide into small groups to practice counting in Russian.

Study the adult introduction to the food of Russia in Gregory and Rita Plotkin's *Cooking the Russian Way*. Share interesting food habits of the Russians with the children. Tell them about breakfast, dinner, and supper in Russia as you show the illustrations. Prepare a food or drink such as *Kompot* for the class to taste.

8. Read Lenny Hort's *The Boy Who Held Back the Sea* to the class. Let the students discuss why they know the setting of the story is not the United States, even though the text does not indicate a place. In what country does the class think the story is set? Are there clues in Thomas Locker's illustrations that suggest a setting? Guide students to notice the windmills and dikes as indications of the Netherlands. Locate the Netherlands on a map. Ask a committee to go to the library media center to find out why the people of the Netherlands build and maintain dikes. Let them report their findings to the class.

9. Before reading Riki Levinson's *Our Home Is the Sea*, locate Hong Kong on the map. Tell the class they will hear four new words: "amah," "congee," "sampan," and "tram." The words are defined on the back of the Title Page, but ask the class to try to decide the meaning from the context. Also ask them to notice the illustrations and be able to share anything they learn about life in Hong Kong. After reading the book, let the students discuss the new words. What is life like in Hong Kong? How did the land region affect the parents' choice of a home? What does the boy plan for his future work and why was that his choice? How do we know the boy was a good student in school?

10. Before reading Ann Morris's *Hats Hats Hats* let the children suggest reasons for wearing hats. Read the book to the class. Go back through the illustrations and for every hat representing a country outside the United States, point out the country and continent on the map and share the brief information given by the author in the index.

Ask the children to pick another country not represented in the book. Take the class to the library media center and, with the help of the library media specialist, encourage students to locate a book that has an illustration of a hat unique to the selected country. Have them consider why the people in the country wear that particular kind of hat. Let students share their findings with the class. Students will want to consider the weather, the wearer's occupation, and the desire for personal attractiveness.

Celebrations

STUDENT OBJECTIVES:

1. Identify the origins of customs associated with familiar holidays.
2. Discuss traditions and food used to celebrate holidays around the world.
3. Share holiday poetry, stories, and folklore unique to various countries around the world.
4. Invent a holiday that would be a meaningful celebration.

RECOMMENDED READINGS:

Ancona, George. *Dancing Is.* E. P. Dutton, 1981.
Photographs and brief text celebrate dancing around the world. (Objective 2)

Anno, Mitsumasa. *All in a Day.* Philomel, 1986.
Peace and similarities are the themes as distinguished artists share New Year's Day in eight different countries, showing how time and climate affect activities. (Objective 2)

Baylor, Byrd. *I'm in Charge of Celebrations.* Illustrated by Peter Parnall. Charles Scribner's Sons, 1986.
In poetic language Baylor shares special celebrations of nature that are meaningful to her. (Objective 4)

Brown, Tricia. *Chinese New Year.* Illustrated by Fran Ortiz. Henry Holt, 1987.
Photographs enhance the simple text that describes the customs associated with the Chinese New Year celebration in San Francisco's Chinatown. (Objectives 1 and 2)

Burns, Diane L. *Arbor Day.* Illustrated by Kathy Rogers. Carolrhoda, 1989.
Discusses Arbor Day and describes how it is celebrated around the world. (Objectives 1 and 4)

Cohen, Barbara. *Molly's Pilgrim*. Illustrated by Michael J. Deraney. Lothrop, Lee & Shepard, 1983.
When Molly is given the assignment of making a Pilgrim doll for her school's Thanksgiving display, her mother makes a doll dressed as a Jewish immigrant who left Russia seeking religious freedom. (Objective 2)

de Paola, Tomie. *The Family Christmas Tree Book*. Holiday House, 1980.
As a family selects and decorates their Christmas tree, they discuss its origin. (Objectives 1, 2, and 3)

Ets, Marie Hall and Labastida, Aurora. *Nine Days to Christmas*. Viking, 1959.
A young girl in Mexico gets to choose her first Christmas piñata. (Objectives 1 and 2)

Kelley, Emily. *April Fool's Day*. Illustrated by C. A. Nobens. Carolrhoda, 1983.
Suggests different theories about the origins of April Fool's Day and some of the pranks played over the years. (Objectives 1, 2, and 3)

————. *Christmas around the World*. Illustrated by Priscilla Kiedrowski. Carolrhoda, 1986.
Focuses on Christmas customs in seven countries with brief accounts of four others. (Objective 2)

————. *Happy New Year*. Illustrated by Priscilla Kiedrowski. Carolrhoda, 1984.
Simple text describes New Year's customs in a number of countries in the world. (Objective 2)

Kroll, Steven. *Oh, What a Thanksgiving!* Illustrated by S. D. Schindler. Scholastic, 1988.
David's teacher helps him appreciate his own Thanksgiving rather than wishing he were in Plymouth. (Objectives 1 and 2)

Polacco, Patricia. *Rechenka's Eggs*. Philomel, 1988.
Babushka befriends an injured goose and is repaid with two miracles. (Objectives 2 and 3)

Prelutsky, Jack. *It's Thanksgiving*. Illustrated by Marylin Hafner. Greenwillow, 1982.
Thanksgiving poems identify many of the customs in a humorous way. (Objectives 2 and 3)

Robbins, Ruth. *Baboushka and the Three Kings*. Illustrated by Nicolas Sidjakov. Houghton Mifflin, 1960.
Presents the Russian folktale of an old woman who leaves precious gifts for children each Christmas season. (Objectives 1 and 3)

GROUP INTRODUCTORY ACTIVITY:

Preparation: Locate Byrd Baylor's *I'm in Charge of Celebrations* and a calendar that identifies the dates of national holidays.

Focus: Tell the class that people like to remember important events with yearly celebrations. Show a calendar and discuss the date of several selected holidays. What special event in America's history is celebrated July 4th? Why are the birthdays of George Washington, Abraham Lincoln, and Martin Luther King celebrated as national holidays? Guide the discussion to cover special family celebrations like birthdays and anniversaries.

Objective: In order to invent a holiday that would be a meaningful celebration, ask the students if they would like to celebrate more events than the ones they already have. Tell them Byrd Baylor's book *I'm in Charge of Celebrations* is about the author's personal celebrations.

Guided Activity: Read the book to the class. How many celebrations did the narrator give herself last year? Of those 108, what celebrations did she choose to discuss? What do the students suppose some of Baylor's other celebrations could have been? Go through the book recalling the dates of each celebration. Select a student to write the name of each special holiday on its date in the calendar.

Extending Activity: Have the students write and illustrate an additional episode for the book based on a special event in their lives they would like to remember with a yearly celebration. Have students select a name and date for their celebrations, and let each write the name on the appropriate date in the calendar. Bind their writing into a class book titled *I'm in Charge of Celebrations*.

FOLLOW-UP ACTIVITIES FOR TEACHER AND STUDENTS TO SHARE:

1. Ask the class to speculate about why people dance. List their ideas on the chalkboard. Read George Ancona's *Dancing Is* to the class. After reading the book, go back to selected illustrations of dances around the world. Name the dance, locate on the globe the country represented, and briefly describe the dance to the children using the information in the appendix. After sharing the selected dances, ask students what reasons for dancing they would like to add to the chalkboard list.

   As a follow-up, ask the physical education teacher or a local dance group to demonstrate a traditional dance and perhaps teach it to the children.

2. Share the pictures and brief text of Mitsumasa Anno's *All in a Day* with the class. Locate the eight countries on a map. Let students take turns describing how the children in each celebrated the New Year. What activities were the same or

similar? Why do the students suppose there are differences in the ways the New Year is celebrated?

3. Introduce Tricia Brown's *Chinese New Year* by asking the class on what date the people in the United States usually celebrate New Year's Day. After the class responds with January 1, locate San Francisco on the map. Tell the children that Tricia Brown lives in San Francisco's Chinatown and that this book describes the celebration of the Chinese New Year. Ask them to listen to find out when the Chinese New Year is and to notice other customs associated with the holiday. After reading the book, ask the children to recall in what months the New Year may be celebrated. Then go back through the book and show the children each photograph. Ask them to describe the custom associated with that illustration.

   As a follow-up, have the children replicate the lucky character sign seen in many homes, using a felt-tip pen and a diamond-shaped piece of red construction paper. Each may be posted on a white paper doily and displayed.

4. Before reading *Arbor Day* by Diane Burns, ask the class if any know how Arbor Day is celebrated. If needed, show them the cover of the book which pictures children planting a tree. Tell the class to listen as you read the book to find out how Arbor Day was celebrated in the past as well as today. After reading the book, ask the children if they recall the state in which the holiday began. If they do not recall Nebraska, read page 25 again. Locate the state on the map.

   Ask the children why Arbor Day is celebrated in the spring or fall rather than the winter. Have them suggest what tree they would plant if they were celebrating Arbor Day as a school project. Ask them to justify their answers. Let them recall other countries that celebrate Arbor Day. Reread pages 30 and 31 if needed. Locate those countries on the map or globe.

   Ask the children to think about creating a new celebration called Flower Day to make their state beautiful. Discuss what flower they might wish to plant. List the suggestions on the chalkboard and have committees of children research the listed flowers in the library media center to find out if those flowers would grow in their state's climate. Urge the children to make pictures of the flowers that are appropriate and decide on a specific day for celebration. Post the pictures on a bulletin board labeled "Let's Celebrate Flowers."

5. Before reading *Molly's Pilgrim* by Barbara Cohen, ask the students to define the word "pilgrim." After several students

have offered suggestions, have one student read the dictionary definition. After discussing the definition, have the students tell how they think a pilgrim should dress. Ask the class to keep that discussion in mind as you read the story. After reading the book, ask the students if they have changed their minds about the way pilgrims dress. What do they think now? In the story, Molly's family were Russian Jews. What other pilgrims, besides those who settled in Massachusetts, have come to the United States? What pilgrims have come in recent years? Lead students to mention Southeast Asian and Spanish-speaking immigrants.

Let the students make and costume pilgrim dolls using clothes pins or cardboard figures. Encourage the students to make dolls representing a variety of immigrant groups in addition to traditional pilgrims. Students may want to visit the library media center to research the traditional costumes of their pilgrims.

6. Read Tomie de Paola's *The Family Christmas Tree Book* to the class. Let the children recall the origins of the various customs associated with the tree. Locate Germany on a map and ask students which of the customs came from there. Why did President Teddy Roosevelt not have a Christmas tree one year? Can the students think of ways a family can enjoy the Christmas tree tradition without cutting down a live tree? Let the children make a Christmas ornament to place on a classroom or community tree. They may want to string popcorn and cranberries, make decorative cookies, or copy the angel ornament for which directions are given in the book.

7. Before reading Marie Hall Ets and Aurora Labastida's *Nine Days to Christmas*, point out Mexico on a globe. Can the children speculate about Mexico's climate from its location on the globe? How might Mexico's warm climate affect the way people there celebrate Christmas? Read the book. In what ways are the Christmas customs in Mexico the same as those in the United States? In what ways are they different?

Make a list of the activities at Ceci's posada. Using the list as a guide, let the students plan a class posada. For the celebration, the students can make a star-shaped pinata using cardboard and papier-mache.

8. In the week before April 1, read Emily Kelley's *April Fools' Day* aloud. Ask students to recall the different suggestions about how April Fools' Day began. List their responses on the chalkboard. After April 1, have the students write paragraphs telling how they tricked or were tricked by somebody.

9. Read to the class the two introductory pages of Emily Kelley's *Christmas around the World.* Assign small groups of two or three students to read about Christmas in a specific country covered in the book. Send each group to the library media center to see if they can find additional information about Christmas in their assigned country. When the groups have finished the reading and research, have them locate the countries on the map and report to the class about the Christmas customs. As a class discussion, let the students select the country they would prefer to visit at Christmas and tell why they made the choice.

10. Read Emily Kelley's *Happy New Year* to the students. Let them locate the countries mentioned on the map and recall specific New Year customs of each. Which do they feel are the most unusual customs? Do any customs in Equador and Iran remind the students of other holidays in the United States? With the students make wassail according to the book's recipe. Invite the music teacher to share the wassail with the class. Perhaps she or he will help the students learn "Here's to Thee, Old Apple Tree!" After they have learned the song, let the students select a tree in the school yard and pretend it is an apple tree. They can then be "howlers," sing the apple tree song, and "wassail the fruit trees" as boys do in England on New Year's Day.

11. Before reading Steven Kroll's *Oh, What a Thanksgiving!*, write the title "Thanksgiving Today" on the chalkboard. Ask the class to share what their families do on Thanksgiving. List the responses. Write the title "Thanksgiving in Plymouth Colony" on the chalkboard and ask the students to listen as you read for details of the first Thanksgiving. After reading the book, let students recall the details of that first Thanksgiving celebration and list their responses on the chalkboard. Would the students prefer to be in Plymouth Colony or their own homes for Thanksgiving? Urge them to refer to the two lists for reasons to support their decisions.

12. To introduce Patricia Polacco's *Rechenka's Eggs*, ask the children if they have ever painted eggs. For which holiday did they do this? Locate Russia on the map and tell the class they will hear the story of a special Easter Festival that turned into a miracle for Babushka. Prepare them to listen for the meanings of Russian words that are new to them. Read the first sentence and ask what a "dacha" is. After completing the story, talk about the meaning of other words new to the children. Why did the goose replace Babushka's eggs? Why was the feather-bed quilt a perfect prize for Babushka to win? If the story continued, what might happen

to Babushka and Rechenka's baby? Let each child paint a beautiful paper egg they think Babushka could use as a pattern for future eggs she might paint.

13. Share the poems in Jack Prelutsky's *It's Thanksgiving* with the class. Listen to Jack Prelutsky reading these poems on the *It's Thanksgiving* tape (Scholastic, 1987). Discuss the customs Prelutsky wrote about that are typical of many families. Have the students find other short poems about a holiday, and let each select a favorite. Duplicate the selected poems and let the students draw an appropriate border. Compile a book titled "Favorite Holiday Poems." Let the students first practice, then read their chosen poems into a tape recorder. Leave the class's book and tape in the listening center for the children to enjoy throughout the year.

14. Read Ruth Robbins's *Baboushka and the Three Kings*. Discuss the ending of the story. Does the Russian custom of Baboushka's Christmas visits remind the children of any Christmas custom in the United States? With the help of the music teacher, let the class learn the song at the end of the book. Assign several students parts, and let them pantomime the story as the rest of the class sings the song.

Chapter 3
Fourth Grade/Fifth Grade

Early America

STUDENT OBJECTIVES:

1. Describe the arrival of the Indians, Europeans, and Africans in North America.
2. Discuss the way of life of Native Americans living in what is now the United States when the Europeans first settled in the New World.
3. Explore the relationship between the Native Americans and the earliest European settlers.
4. Assess the difficulties of people who came to America in bondage.
5. Discuss the way of life of Europeans after settling in America.

RECOMMENDED READINGS:

Avi. *Encounter at Easton.* Pantheon, 1980.
    In this sequel to *Night Journeys*, two indentured servants seek security in a Pennsylvania town. (Objective 4)

————. *Night Journeys.* Pantheon, 1979.
    Two escaped indentured servants receive help from a 12-year-old Pennsylvania boy. (Objective 4)

Corwin, Judith Hoffman. *Colonial American Crafts: The Home.* Franklin Watts, 1989.
    Describes life in the colonies between 1607 and 1776 and gives recipes and instructions for making crafts. (Objective 5)

Forest, Heather. *The Baker's Dozen: A Colonial American Tale.* Illustrated by Susan Gaber. Harcourt Brace Jovanovich, 1988.
In 1655, a Dutch American baker learns the value of generosity to his customers and begins an American tradition. (Objective 5)

Fritz, Jean. *The Double Life of Pocahontas.* Illustrated by Ed Young. G. P. Putnam's Sons, 1983.
Life in Jamestown and relations between the Indians and white settlers are explored in a biography of Pocahontas. (Objectives 1, 2, and 3)

Gibbons, Gail. *From Path to Highway.* Thomas Y. Crowell, 1986.
Gives the 500 year history of the Boston Post Road. (Objective 5)

Krensky, Stephen. *Who Really Discovered America?* Illustrated by Steve Sullivan. Scholastic, 1987.
Discusses the individuals and groups of people who first came to the North American continent. (Objective 1)

Sewall, Marcia. *The Pilgrims of Plimoth.* Atheneum, 1986.
The journey to the colony and the role of men, women, and children in the society are described in the language of the times. (Objectives 1, 2, 3, and 5)

Siegel, Beatrice. *Fur Trappers and Traders.* Illustrated by William Sauts Bock. Walker, 1987.
The beaver helped shape American history and the relations between the Pilgrims and the Indians. (Objectives 2, 3, and 5)

Speare, Elizabeth George. *The Sign of the Beaver.* Houghton Mifflin, 1983.
The Indians insure his survival as 13-year-old Matt guards his family's cabin in the Maine wilderness. (Objectives 2, 3, and 5)

Tunis, Edwin. *Indians.* Rev. ed. Thomas Y. Crowell, 1979.
A detailed description of Indian culture in North America before the arrival of the Europeans. (Objective 2)

Wolfson, Evelyn. *From Abenaki to Zuni.* Illustrated by William Sauts Bock. Walker, 1988.
Arranged alphabetically, 68 North American Indian tribes and their cultures are described. (Objectives 1 and 2)

Yates, Elizabeth. *Amos Fortune, Free Man.* Illustrated by Nora S. Unwin. E. P. Dutton, 1950.
Biography of an African prince who, after years of slavery in America, was able to buy his own freedom and that of others. (Objective 4)

GROUP INTRODUCTORY ACTIVITY:

Preparation: Locate *Indians* by Edwin Tunis. Acquire a package of 3" × 5" index cards and a file box.

Focus: On the chalkboard write the words "atlatl," "babiche," "chungke yard," "flint knapping," "goyemshi," "labret," "manitou," "otekoa," "quamash," and "wampum." Ask the students if they know the meaning of any of these terms. After accepting responses, ask how one could go about finding the meaning of those not defined. If looking in the dictionary is mentioned, select several students to try that method, each using a different dictionary. Students should be able to find some, but not all, of the terms. Let them read any definitions found.

Objective: In order to discuss the way of life of Native Americans living in what is now the United States when the Europeans first settled in the New World, introduce *Indians* by Edwin Tunis. Explain that it is a book that uses all the terms on the chalkboard and many more in a detailed description of the daily lives of Indians who lived in North America before the Europeans came. Tell students that the terms are listed in the Index, and a definition or description of the term can be found on the indicated pages.

Guided Activity: To demonstrate that definitions can be deduced from the text, select a term and look it up in the Index. Go to the indicated page and read aloud the paragraphs containing the term. Let the students suggest a definition after hearing the term used in context. Write the term on a 3″ × 5″ card along with the suggested definition.

Ask another student to select a different term from the list, look it up in the Index, and read aloud the paragraphs indicated. Let the class again formulate a definition after hearing the term used in context. Have the student write the term and its definition. As time allows, let other students follow the procedure with different terms. Make Tunis's book available for the students to read. Urge them to participate in the suggested extending activity.

Extending Activity: Let the students compile a card glossary of new terms they find in *Indians*. Direct them to scan the Index, find an interesting word, and follow the process demonstrated in class to find the meaning of the word and to prepare a card. Let them place their cards alphabetically in a file box. From time to time, let students share their cards with the class. Eager students may want to continue the project throughout the "Early America" unit.

FOLLOW-UP ACTIVITIES FOR TEACHER AND STUDENTS TO SHARE:

1. Introduce Avi's *Night Journeys* by reading the first three chapters. Have the class discuss the meaning of the words "indentured servant." Why would indentured servants try to escape? If the students do not mention the desire to be free, lead them to that reason. Why did Peter York want to go along to hunt for the two escaped indentured servants?

    Ask a volunteer to read the book and report back to the

class what happens to the escapees. Tell the reader to determine why Peter changes his attitude during the search. Ask a committee to go to the library media center and find more information about indentured servants. Ask them to prepare a class report. After both reports have been given, ask students to consider freedom in modern times. What people in the world are still seeking freedom?

2. After the class has been introduced to Avi's *Night Journeys*, heard a report on the remainder of the story, and discussed research on the topic of indentured servants, introduce Avi's *Encounter at Easton* by reading the first three chapters. Let the class discuss Mr. Tolivar's character and how they would feel about being indentured to him. Why did the two children try to escape to Easton? Ask a member of the class to read the book and share with the class what happens to the two children.

3. Introduce Judith Hoffman Corwin's *Colonial American Crafts: The Home* by reading the chapter "The Home." After the reading, have the students recall facts about home life in the colonial period. Suggest that each member of the class make some item indicative of colonial home life, such as a treasure box, paper costumes, or a cross-stitch alphabet sampler. Perhaps someone would like to make a "Journey Cake" at home and bring it to share with the class.

4. Before reading Heather Forest's *The Baker's Dozen: A Colonial American Tale*, ask the class if they know what the title means. Tell them the story was inspired by an early Albany, New York baker who began the custom of a "baker's dozen" in 1655. Read the book. What does the story have to say about honest and dishonest business practices? How are these ideas applicable today? Have a committee go to the media center and find more information or any stories about the Dutch settlement of New Amsterdam. Ask the committee to present their findings to the class.

5. Introduce Jean Fritz's *The Double Life of Pocahontas* by asking the students to recall what they know about the Jamestown colony or about Pocahontas. Tell the class that this biography of Pocahontas clearly identifies the problems of survival faced by the Jamestown settlers and the dilemma of the Indians as they were forced to share their land.

   Read the first chapter aloud to the class. How do the students think the Indians must have felt when the white settlers arrived? How would we respond if strangers tried to take over our city or town? Be sure to check the notes at the end of the book before reading each chapter to see if there is information that should be shared with the class.

After reading chapter 2, let the class discuss the problems of survival faced by the colonists and the political struggles engaged in by their leaders. How did Pocahontas get involved in the conflict between the white settlers and the Indians?

Read chapters 3 and 4 to the class. Why was the year known as the "Starving Time?" How must the Indians have felt as they saw the first ship leave and then another strange ship arrive? What happened to Pocahontas as the white settlers and Indians continued their conflict?

Read chapter 5 and the Epilogue. Ask the class to discuss what they learned about life in the Jamestown colony from hearing *The Double Life of Pocahontas*. As a follow-up, ask each member of the class to complete one of the individual activities relating to the book.

6. Before reading Gail Gibbons's *From Path to Highway*, locate Boston and New York City on the map. Tell the class the book gives the history of travel between those two cities. Ask them to listen for the meanings of "postrider" and "corduroy roads," the origin of the word "turnpike," and the term "iron horse." After reading the book, share the brief descriptions of famous travelers who used the three routes between New York and Boston. Let the class discuss the new terms, the number of days required to travel between the two cities in 1673, and the different modes of transportation used during the 300 years. Have students build vehicles from small boxes that represent the development of transportation along the road.

7. Before introducing Stephen Krensky's *Who Really Discovered America?* to the class, write the book's title at the top of a sheet of butcher paper. Ask the children if they know the answer to the title's question. List their responses. Read Krensky's book aloud. As chapters are completed, let the class discuss possible answers provided in the text and add to the butcher paper list. After the book is completed, let the class mark out any of their introductory answers that have not been documented in the book. Discuss how each of those remaining on the list contributed to or affected the way of life of today's Americans.

8. Before reading Marcia Sewall's *The Pilgrims of Plimoth*, write "The Language of the Pilgrims" on the chalkboard. Tell the students the book is written in the English of the 1600s, and they should note any terms they do not understand so the terms can be discussed later. After reading the section "The Pilgrims," let the class suggest unusual expres-

sions they heard. List their responses on the chalkboard and discuss the meaning of each. Also have the students discuss the important leaders of the Plimoth community and the Pilgrims' struggle for survival.

After reading the section "Menfolk," lead a discussion of the role of the men in the colony and contrast that role with the one of men today. Again discuss words and expressions that are no longer used. Add those discussed to the chalkboard list.

Read "Womenfolk." Let the class identify tasks accepted by women, household items, and the herbs used for medicine. Many terms such as "pipkins and pottles" will need to be explored, using the glossary as necessary. Again add these to the list on the chalkboard.

After reading the last sections "Children and Youngfolk" and "The Plantation," discuss the work of children and their recreational activities. What was important for the children to learn in colonial Plimoth? Would that be valuable information today?

9. Introduce Beatrice Siegel's *Fur Trappers and Traders* by reading pages 21–26 in which three questions are answered: (1) Why did the Pilgrims have to depend on the fur trade?, (2) How did the English merchants help the Pilgrims?, (3) What happened to the Pilgrims' first cargo? Let the class discuss the answers to these questions. Pose two additional questions regarding the relationship of the Indians and European settlers: (1) How did the Dutch, French, and the Puritans compete for the fur trade?, (2) Were the Indians helped by their part in the fur trade business? Ask a student to read the book and share the answers to these questions with the class.

10. Introduce Elizabeth George Speare's *The Sign of the Beaver* by locating Maine on the map and explaining that eighteenth century Maine is the setting for the story. Read the first two chapters. Discuss the plans Matt's family had made in 1768 as they figured out how the move to the Maine territory could be accomplished. What type of house did Matt and his father build? What warnings did his father give Matt before going back to pick up the rest of the family? Let the class discuss how Matt must have felt after his father left. What circumstances might cause parents to have to leave their children alone in a strange place today?

Suggest to the class that you will locate additional copies of the book through interlibrary loan if any would like to read the book and participate in a group discussion of the problems Matt faced. Let those who volunteer share copies that have been located. When all have read the book, lead a discussion of the challenges Matt faced, how the Indians helped him, and what the two boys learned from each other.

11. Introduce Evelyn Wolfson's *From Abenaki to Zuni* by locating on a map of the United States where the Abenaki originally lived. Ask the class to listen carefully as you read about that tribe in order to discuss interesting facts about their homes, food, tribal customs, and how their life was changed by the coming of the Europeans. After reading about and discussing the Abenaki, ask each student to examine the map in the front of the book and choose a tribe on which each would like to report. As students read the appropriate section in the book, have them record interesting facts in the four categories used in discussing the Abenaki.

12. Tell the class that Elizabeth Yates's *Amos Fortune, Free Man* is the biography of an African prince who was captured, brought to America in a slave ship, and sold as a slave in 1725. Read the first two chapters aloud. Let the class discuss the reason why the slave traders chose that particular time to attack the village. Why did the slavers treat the captives so cruelly on board ship? What did the slavers want the Africans to forget? Ask a student to volunteer to read the book and share with the class what happened to At-mun as he searched for freedom.

FOLLOW-UP ACTIVITIES FOR INDIVIDUALS OR SMALL GROUPS:

1. After hearing Jean Fritz's *The Double Life of Pocahontas*, get Ingri d'Aulaire's *Pocahontas* (Doubleday, 1946) from the school or public library. Read the book and write a paragraph about any differences in the life of Pocahontas that were recorded in the two books. Write a second short paragraph telling which book gave the most useful information and why you made that choice.

2. After hearing Jean Fritz's *The Double Life of Pocahontas*, go to the library media center and find information about life in the Jamestown colony. Write a paragraph telling any facts you learned that Fritz chose not to record in her biography of Pocahontas.

3. List the places located on the map at the back of Jean Fritz's *The Double Life of Pocahontas*. Write a sentence about one event that happened in Pocahontas's life at each

location you listed. Check an atlas to see if those places are
still on the map today.

4. After hearing Jean Fritz's *The Double Life of Pocahontas*,
write a newspaper account of the wedding of Pocahontas
and John Rolfe. The article should answer the questions
"who," "what," "when," and "where" about the event.

5. After hearing Jean Fritz's *The Double Life of Pocahontas*,
research life in Powhatan's village. Draw a picture or make
a model of the village.

6. After hearing Jean Fritz's *The Double Life of Pocahontas*,
research life in the Jamestown colony. Draw a picture or
make a model of a typical home.

7. Working with a partner, each of you select a character from
Jean Fritz's *The Double Life of Pocahontas*. Write a dialog
that might have taken place between the two characters.
Perform the dialog for the class. You may want to wear
costumes for the presentation.

8. Read pages 7–20 in Beatrice Siegel's *Fur Trappers and
Traders*. Write a short paragraph telling why the English
were so interested in the beaver.

9. Look up "moccasin game" or "plumstone game" in the
Index of *Indians* by Edwin Tunis. Explain the rules and
demonstrate how to play the game to the class.

10. Use the Table of Contents in the front of Edwin Tunis's
Indians to find the description of the clothes worn by one
group of Indians. Examine the illustrations and read the text
to find out what materials were used in making the clothes,
how they were decorated, and how climate affected the way
clothing was made. Did the clothing change from summer
to winter? How was the clothing different for men and
women? Make figures of the Indians and patterns of their
clothing, using poster board for the Indian figures and thin-
ner paper for the clothes. Leave tabs on the clothes so they
can be put on and taken off the figures. Share with the class
and report facts you have learned.

11. Use the Index of Edwin Tunis's *Indians* to find information
about the foods eaten by three different groups of Indians.
List all of the foods identified for each group. In a written
paragraph tell what foods the three groups had in common
and which ones we still eat today.

12. Read *Amos Fortune, Free Man* by Elizabeth Yates. Write a
paragraph explaining why you feel the author won the
Newbery Medal for this book.

13. After reading Elizabeth Yates's *Amos Fortune, Free Man*, select the scene when Amos arrives in Jaffrey and meets the constable. With a friend play out the scene for the class.

Becoming a Nation

STUDENT OBJECTIVES:

1. Identify the reasons Americans sought independence from Great Britain.
2. Describe the people and events associated with the Revolutionary War period.
3. Describe the people and events associated with writing the Constitution and establishing the new government.
4. Give examples of the ways people demonstrated a change in cultural attitude from English to American.

RECOMMENDED READINGS:

Adler, David A. *Thomas Jefferson, Father of Our Democracy*. Illustrated by Jacqueline Garrick. Holiday House, 1987.
Recounts the many accomplishments of Jefferson but concentrates on his political career. (Objectives 2, 3, and 4)

Avi. *The Fighting Ground*. J. B. Lippincott, 1984.
Thirteen-year-old Jonathan gets a new view of the conflict as he spends 24 hours fighting in the Revolutionary War. (Objective 2)

Carter, Alden R. *At the Forge of Liberty*. Franklin Watts, 1988.
Gives a brief overview of the Revolutionary War's causes, leaders, and events. (Objective 2)

Cobblestone. Vol. 10, No. 9. (September 1989) Entire issue.
A thematic issue about Thomas Jefferson. (Objectives 1, 2, 3, and 4)

Collier, James Lincoln and Collier, Christopher. *Jump Ship to Freedom*. Delacorte, 1981.
A 14-year-old slave escapes his dishonest master to cash his father's Revolutionary War notes and buy freedom for his family. (Objectives 2 and 3)

Davis, Burke. *Black Heroes of the American Revolution*. Harcourt Brace Jovanovich, 1976.
Briefly describes the contribution of African-Americans who participated in the struggle for the country's independence from England. (Objective 2)

Ferris, Jeri. *What Do You Mean?* Illustrated by Steve Michaels. Carolrhoda, 1988.
Shows how Noah Webster, a poor farm boy, became a teacher and writer who influenced the education of the new Americans. (Objectives 1, 2, 3, and 4)

Fisher, Leonard Everett. *Monticello.* Holiday House, 1988.
Jefferson's dream home is described from planning to occupancy and from deterioration to restoration. (Objective 3)

Fritz, Jean. *The Cabin Faced West.* Illustrated by Feodor Rojankovsky. Viking, 1958.
Ann Hamilton is discouraged with her family's western Pennsylvania home until they entertain General Washington. (Objective 2)

——. *Can't You Make Them Behave, King George?* Illustrated by Tomie de Paola. Coward, McCann & Geoghegan, 1972.
The reaction of England's King George III to the American Revolution is an important aspect of this biography. (Objectives 1 and 2)

——. *George Washington's Breakfast.* Illustrated by Paul Galdone. Coward-McCann, 1969.
George Washington Allen chooses many methods to research what his namesake ate for breakfast. (Objectives 2 and 3)

——. *Shh! We're Writing the Constitution.* Illustrated by Tomie de Paola. G. P. Putnam's Sons, 1987.
Describes the problems in writing the Constitution and its final ratification. (Objective 3)

——. *Where Was Patrick Henry on the 29th of May?* Illustrated by Margot Tomes. Coward, McCann & Geoghegan, 1975.
Describes the important periods in Henry's life with emphasis on his service to his country after age 25. (Objectives 1 and 2)

Hilton, Suzanne. *We the People: The Way We Were 1783-1793.* Westminster, 1981.
Describes life in the first 10 years of the new nation. (Objective 4)

Lawson, Robert. *Ben and Me.* Little, Brown, 1939.
A poor church mouse takes up residence in Franklin's fur cap and assists in many accomplishments credited to Franklin. (Objectives 1 and 2)

McGovern, Ann. *The Secret Soldier.* Illustrated by Ann Grifalconi. Four Winds, 1975, 1987.
The biography of Deborah Sampson who disguised herself as a man and served in the Revolutionary War. (Objective 2)

Roop, Peter and Roop, Connie. *Buttons for General Washington.* Illustrated by Peter Hanson. Carolrhoda, 1986.
Describes in simple vocabulary how a 14-year-old Philadelphia spy carries messages written in code to Washington's camp. (Objective 2)

Siegel, Beatrice. *George and Martha Washington at Home in New York.* Illustrated by Frank Aloise. Four Winds, 1989.
Government and social activities are highlighted as the Washingtons spend 16 months in the nation's first capital. (Objective 3)

GROUP INTRODUCTORY ACTIVITY:

Preparation: Locate the September 1989 issue of *Cobblestone* magazine which is dedicated to the life of Thomas Jefferson. If your school's library media center does not have back issues of *Cobblestone*, request the issue through interlibrary loan. If you want your own copy, send for a catalog of back issues to Cobblestone Publishing, Inc., 30 Grove Street, Peterborough, NH 03458.

On a roll of shelf paper make a timeline of the important events in Thomas Jefferson's life using the dates and events found on page five of the timeline in the *Cobblestone* issue. When making the timeline, leave space so that additional events can be added.

Focus: Display the timeline and tell students that Jefferson played an important role in some of the most memorable events in the history of our country. Briefly discuss the items listed on the timeline.

Objective: To address the objective of describing the people and events associated with the Revolutionary War period, tell the class they will discover many events that should be added to the timeline as they study the life of Thomas Jefferson and the other people and events associated with the early history of the United States.

As an overview of Jefferson's life, read aloud "Thomas Jefferson: A Man of Knowledge," pp. 4–5. Ask students to recall a date that can be added to the timeline. If necessary, reread the sentences about George Washington's taking the presidential oath and add April 30, 1789, to the timeline. Ask students to discuss what Jefferson did in his youth to prepare himself for adult life. What are some of the things he accomplished as an adult?

Guided Activity: Tell students that they are going to read a play about Jefferson's first activities in public service. Assign parts in the play "From Lawyer to Patriot," pp. 9–14. So that everyone can participate, you may want to assign several students to read the roles that occur in more than one scene. Set the stage for each of the five scenes and allow time for the students in each scene to practice reading their lines.

After Act 1, Scene 1, is presented, ask students to discuss what the British Parliament did to anger the Americans. Why were the Americans angry with King George III? What are some of Patrick Henry's character traits? Add the events of May 30, 1765, to the timeline.

After Act 1, Scene 2, have students discuss the difference of opinion between Peter Randolph and Patrick Henry.

Before Act II, Scene 1, point out 1768 on the timeline and identify it as the date Thomas Jefferson was first elected to public office. After the presentation, ask students to discuss the Townshend

Act. Have students discuss the two declarations about taxation and court trials of Americans made by the House of Burgesses.

Let students present Act II, Scene 2. What did Thomas Jefferson, George Washington, Patrick Henry, and others agree to do when they signed the Virginia Association paper?

Before presenting the final scene, identify Williamsburg, Virginia and Boston, Massachusetts on the map. After the reading, discuss the Boston Tea Party, the Boston Port Act, and the Virginians' response to the act.

Extending Activity: Encourage students to add to the timeline throughout the "Becoming a Nation" unit and urge each student to complete one of the individual activities suggested for the Thomas Jefferson issue of *Cobblestone*.

FOLLOW-UP ACTIVITIES FOR TEACHER AND STUDENTS TO SHARE:

1. Before introducing David A. Adler's *Thomas Jefferson, Father of Our Democracy*, draw a tombstone on a sheet of butcher paper. Find the epitaph Jefferson wrote for himself on the last page of the book and print it on the butcher paper tombstone, leaving space for more lines to be written below it. Read the epitaph aloud and tell the class that Thomas Jefferson should be remembered for many other accomplishments besides the three he wanted mentioned on his tombstone. Encourage the students to read Adler's biography of Jefferson and add accomplishments to the tombstone list that they feel are significant.

2. Introduce Alden R. Carter's *At the Forge of Liberty* by reading chapter 1. Ask the class to discuss the causes of the Revolution. Why was it called the Accidental War? Check to see if the date of the Declaration of Independence is on the timeline the class has prepared. Ask the students to suggest events from chapter 1 that should be listed. Continue the timeline with their suggestions. Assign each interested student to read about one of the following: Germantown, Valley Forge, Monmouth Court House, Bonhomme Richard sea battle, Savannah siege, Battle of Charleston, Camden, King's Mountain, Cowpens, Guilford Court House, and Yorktown. When the students have read the assigned section and have written the name of their event in its proper place on the timeline, let them briefly share with the class what they learned.

3. Introduce Burke Davis's *Black Heroes of the American Revolution* by reading the first two pages. Discuss the possible

reasons why the contributions of African-Americans to the Revolutionary War have largely been ignored. To give the heroes the recognition they deserve, encourage each student to scan Davis's collection of short biographies, select a favorite hero, and write a newspaper article about that person's service to the country. Urge students to use a striking headline. Have them post the articles so others will choose a different hero.

4. Introduce Jeri Ferris's *What Do You Mean?* by telling the children that this book is about Noah Webster, a poor farm boy, who grew up to influence American education after the Revolution. Ask if anyone knows who Noah Webster was. Have them consider the title of the book. Might it be a clue to his identity? Tell the students that in the next few days you will read the book aloud as there is much about Noah Webster worth discussing. Read the Introduction and the first two chapters aloud to the class. Let the children discuss what made Noah decide he did not like King George III. Talk about how Noah's school was different from that of the children today. How could Noah's father afford to send him to college? How may poor young people be able to go to college today? How did the Revolutionary War interrupt college life?

   After reading chapters 3 and 4, ask the class to discuss problems Noah encountered in teaching school. Why did Noah feel so desperate to earn money? Why did Noah feel that his spelling book was the "second Declaration of Independence?" Why did he make so little money on his writing?

   Read chapters 5 and 6. Have the children discuss why Washington came to see Noah. What changes did Noah make in his reading book by 1787? Why did Noah think it was important for people to have an American English dictionary?

5. Read Jean Fritz's *George Washington's Breakfast* aloud to the class. Ask them to recall the facts George Allen already knew about George Washington. What methods did he use to find new information? Ask each student to select a well-known person from the period of the Revolutionary War and the writing of the Constitution. Assist students with names if needed. Ask them to go to the library media center and find five interesting facts about that person, including why each is remembered in history. Let the class have a "Guess Whom I'm Describing" session in which they share their list of facts and see if the class members can guess

who is being described. Have each student make an appropriate border for the list and post on the bulletin board.

6. Before introducing Jean Fritz's *Shh! We're Writing the Constitution*, make four columns on the chalkboard under the overall title "The Constitutional Convention." Let the column headings be: "Issues to Be Settled," "Delegate Problems," "Leaders," and "Contributions." After reading a portion of the book each day, let the class decide what entries will be added to each column. The last paragraph in the book suggests that Thomas Jefferson was pleased to hear that a Bill of Rights would be included. Ask a committee to research in the library media center the provisions of the Bill of Rights and report their findings to the class.

   If possible invite a lawyer, judge, or congressman in your community to talk to the class about how the Constitution has worked for the good of the nation for over 200 years.

7. Introduce Suzanne Hilton's *We the People: The Way We Were 1783–1793* by reading chapter 1, "The Americanizing of America," and chapter 10, "Birthing a New Country." Have the class discuss problems of the new nation and ways people tried to show they were Americans and not English. Divide the class into eight committees. Ask each committee to read an assigned chapter about houses, schools, amusements, etc. Ask them to list on butcher paper the 10 most interesting facts they learned. Post their findings on the walls for other class members to share.

8. Before reading Beatrice Siegel's *George and Martha Washington at Home in New York*, ask the class if any of them remember seeing the inauguration of a president on television. Discuss any impressions they have of the event. Tell the class that you are going to read to them a description of George Washington's inauguration. You will expect them to discuss differences between the first and present-day inauguration ceremonies. Read chapter 1 and the first page of chapter 2. Let the class discuss the differences between then and now. Suggest that students may want to read parts of the book and do one of the individual activities about it.

FOLLOW-UP ACTIVITIES FOR INDIVIDUALS OR SMALL GROUPS:

1. Read Avi's *The Fighting Ground*. Write a paragraph describing how Jonathan felt about the war at the first of the story.

List the events that caused him to change his mind and be happy to return home.

2. After reading Avi's *The Fighting Ground*, go to the school's library media center and research facts about the Hessians during the Revolutionary War. Write a paragraph describing the Hessians' role in the war. Write a second paragraph describing Jonathan's skirmish with them.

3. Read Avi's *The Fighting Ground*. Notice that the brief chapters are titled with a time of day. Select 10 of the chapters and give them a short title that hints what will happen in the chapter.

4. Read "Young Tom Jefferson," pp. 6–7, in *Cobblestone*, September 1989. Make a list of the things young Thomas studied in his daily life and in school to become an educated man.

5. Read "A Quiet Room in Philadelphia," pp. 15–18, in *Cobblestone*, September 1989. In the school's library media center find the Declaration of Independence. With three of your friends develop a choral reading of the first three paragraphs, beginning, "When in the course of human events. . .," and ending, ". . .deriving their powers from the consent of the governed." Assign some lines to individual readers, and let the whole group read other lines. Practice before presenting the choral to the class. Introduce the choral with interesting facts you read in the *Cobblestone* article.

6. Read "A Jefferson Chronology," pp. 20-21, in *Cobblestone*, September 1989. Select three dates you think are important in Jefferson's life that are not on the class's timeline. Write the date and its event in the proper place on the timeline.

7. Read "Shaping a Government of the People" and the song "The People's Friend," pp. 27–31, in *Cobblestone*, September 1989. Write a paragraph describing Jefferson's inauguration. Ask the music teacher to help the class learn the song written in praise of Jefferson.

8. Read "Bone Man in the President's House," pp. 33–35, in *Cobblestone*, September 1989. Write a paragraph telling why Jefferson might be called "The Father of Paleontology."

9. Read "Thomas Jefferson: Family Man," pp. 38–41, in *Cobblestone*, September 1989. Reread the schedule Jefferson devised for his daughter Martha. Do you think the schedule is a good idea or too difficult? Pretend you are Martha writing a letter to her father. Tell what you like about the schedule or what you do not like about it.

10. Read *Jump Ship to Freedom* by James and Christopher Collier. Pretend Daniel's friend Birdsey miraculously survived going overboard in the storm, and the two meet years later when they are both old men. Write a conversation the two might have as they discuss their youthful friendship.

11. Read *Jump Ship to Freedom* by James and Christopher Collier and the authors' note "How Much of This Book is True." Peter Fartherscreft was a fictional character, but many Quaker abolitionists were historical figures. In your school's library media center or the public library, find the name of a Quaker abolitionist and write a paragraph about that person's activities.

12. After reading James and Christopher Collier's *Jump Ship to Freedom*, pretend you are Daniel as a young father telling his children about how he freed himself from slavery. Record your story on a cassette tape.

13. Read Leonard Fisher's *Monticello*. Pretend you are a tour guide taking your class through the restored mansion. Give a brief history of the house, showing the pictures of how it deteriorated. Using the pictures, describe the rooms to your class as if you were actually walking through them.

14. Read *The Cabin Faced West* by Jean Fritz. The book ends with Ann's writing in her diary that George Washington was there. However, she was going to write more about the general's visit tomorrow. Write the description of the day's events that Ann will put in her diary.

15. Read Jean Fritz's *The Cabin Faced West*. Write a paragraph explaining why General Washington said he envied Ann.

16. With a friend read Jean Fritz's *Can't You Make Them Behave, King George?* Pretend television was in use during the time of King George III and prepare a television interview. One of you take the part of the television reporter and the other the part of King George III. The interviewer should ask the following questions: (1) Why did you feel the stamp tax was fair?, (2) What was your reaction when the Americans declared their independence?, (3) How did you react to the news that Cornwallis had surrendered at Yorktown?, (4) Why couldn't "you make them behave, King George?" Practice the interview before presenting it to the class.

17. After reading *Where Was Patrick Henry on the 29th of May?* by Jean Fritz, write a paragraph explaining why you think the book was given that title. In the paragraph, tell what Patrick Henry was doing on four specific May 29 dates during his lifetime.

18. Read Jean Fritz's *Where Was Patrick Henry on the 29th of May?* Write a paragraph describing how Patrick Henry learned to be a lawyer. Find out from an adult how lawyers are trained today. Add a second paragraph telling how the two methods of preparation differ.

19. Read Jean Fritz's *Where Was Patrick Henry on the 29th of May?* Answer the following questions about Patrick Henry's most famous speech given on May 23, 1775: (1) Where was the speech given?, (2) Why was he so angry?, (3) What were the last lines that have become so famous?, (4) What were his actions that made the speech particularly dramatic?, (5) How did the people react to the speech?

20. Read Jean Fritz's *Where Was Patrick Henry on the 29th of May?* Memorize the short excerpt given in the book from his famous speech made on May 23, 1775. Present the speech for the class using the gestures described. If possible, dress in costume for the presentation.

21. Read Robert Lawson's *Ben and Me.* Pretend you are Amos writing a letter to your family describing your part in one of Franklin's accomplishments. Be sure to use several small pieces of paper and write using tiny letters.

22. Read Robert Lawson's *Ben and Me.* Then read in a biography of Franklin about one of the accomplishments described by Amos. In a paragraph describe the differences in the two versions.

23. Read Ann McGovern's *The Secret Soldier.* Write a paragraph telling why Deborah Sampson had to wait until 1778 to decide about her future.

24. Read Ann McGovern's *The Secret Soldier.* List three difficulties Deborah Sampson encountered as a woman who enlisted in the Continental army under the name of Robert Shurtliff.

25. Read Peter and Connie Roop's *Buttons for General Washington.* Find Burton Albert's *More Codes for Kids* (Albert Whitman, 1979) or another code book in the media center or public library. Figure out a message about General Howe's troops that John might have taken to General Washington. Write it in code and devise a way John might have carried the message. Share your idea with the class and let them try to break your code.

26. Read chapters 2, 3, and 4 in Beatrice Siegel's *George and Martha Washington at Home in New York.* Pretend you are Martha Washington, and write a letter to a friend describing your arrival in New York and the next day's reception.

27. Read chapters 5, 6, and the last chapter, "Places to Visit," in Beatrice Siegel's *George and Martha Washington at Home in New York.* Write a paragraph comparing New York of 1789 and New York today. You may need to research facts about modern New York in the library media center or public library.

28. Read chapter 9 "Farewell," in Beatrice Siegel's *George and Martha Washington at Home in New York.* Pretend you are a reporter for a New York newspaper writing a front page story of the Washingtons' departure from New York on August 30, 1790. Be sure to cover the "who," "what," "when," and "where" of the event.

The American Frontier

STUDENT OBJECTIVES:

1. Describe the people and events associated with the American West.
2. Discuss American Indian culture in the West.
3. Assess the challenges faced by the pioneers who participated in the western movement.
4. Assess the challenges faced by the Indians as the pioneers moved West.
5. Relate the folklore associated with the West.

RECOMMENDED READINGS:

Anderson, Joan. *Pioneer Children of Appalachia.* Illustrated by George Ancona. Clarion, 1986.
A living history village in West Virginia is the backdrop for a photographic re-creation of pioneer life in Appalachia between 1790 and 1830. (Objective 3)

Cooper, Michael. *Klondike Fever.* Clarion, 1989.
Photographs and brief description highlight the Gold Rush days and the people who left their homes in the States to found the city of Dawson. (Objectives 1 and 3)

Fisher, Leonard Everett. *The Alamo.* Holiday House, 1987.
Presents the history of the building best known for the famous battle in 1836. (Objectives 1 and 3)

Freedman, Russell. *Buffalo Hunt*. Holiday House, 1988.
Paintings by Catlin, Russell, and other artist-adventurers enhance the account of the life of the Great Plains Indians and the importance of the buffalo to their existence. (Objectives 1, 2, 4, and 5)

————. *Children of the Wild West*. Clarion, 1983.
Photographs enhance this presentation of the role of children in the American West from 1840 to the early 1900s. (Objective 1)

————. *Cowboys of the Wild West*. Clarion, 1985.
Old photographs enhance the true account of the life of trail-driving cowboys. (Objective 1)

————. *Indian Chiefs*. Holiday House, 1987.
Biographies of six Indian chiefs who attempted to save their lands and people from the encroachment of white pioneers. (Objectives 1, 2, and 4)

Goble, Paul. *Death of the Iron Horse*. Bradbury, 1987.
Recounts the story of young Cheyenne Indians who, in an act of bravery, derailed and raided a freight train. (Objectives 2 and 4)

Holling, Holling Clancy. *Tree in the Trail*. Houghton Mifflin, 1942.
Recounts the events that surround a cottonwood tree in Kansas that finally became an ox yoke that went to Santa Fe. (Objectives 1, 2, and 3)

Jakes, John. *Susanna of the Alamo*. Illustrated by Paul Bacon. Harcourt Brace Jovanovich, 1986.
Describes the 1836 massacre at the Alamo focusing on Susanna Dickinson, one of the few survivors. (Objectives 1 and 3)

Kellogg, Steven. *Johnny Appleseed*. William Morrow, 1988.
Presents the real life and the tall tale stories of John Chapman who planted apple orchards in the Middle West. (Objectives 1 and 5)

Lawlor, Laurie. *Addie across the Prairie*. Illustrated by Gail Owens. Albert Whitman, 1986.
Despite her unhappiness at leaving friends in Iowa, Addie learns to adjust to life with her family in the Dakota Territory. (Objective 3)

Le Sueur, Meridel. *Little Brother of the Wilderness*. Alfred A. Knopf, 1947.
The biography of Jonathan Chapman known in history as Johnny Appleseed. (Objectives 1, 3, and 5)

MacLachlan, Patricia. *Sarah, Plain and Tall*. Harper & Row, 1985.
Anna and Caleb hope Sarah, their father's mail-order bride, will choose to stay with the family in their prairie home. (Objective 3)

Quackenbush, Robert. *Who Let Muddy Boots into the White House?* Prentice-Hall, 1986.
Biography of how Old Hickory, a War of 1812 hero, became the president of the common man. (Objective 1)

Rounds, Glen. *Mr. Yowder and the Windwagon*. Holiday House, 1983.
Mr. Yowder's attempts to build a prairie schooner with sails end in failure. (Objectives 3 and 5)

Walker, Barbara M. *The Little House Cookbook.* Illustrated by Garth
   Williams. Harper & Row, 1979.
   Descriptions of pioneer foods and cooking are shared, along with recipes
   for foods mentioned in the *Little House* books. (Objective 3)

Wilder, Laura Ingalls. *On the Banks of Plum Creek.* Illustrated by
   Garth Williams. Harper & Row, 1953.
   The life of a pioneer family in Minnesota is described. (Objective 3)

GROUP INTRODUCTORY ACTIVITY:

Preparation: Locate Paul Goble's *Death of the Iron Horse.*

Focus: Ask the students to recall a movie they have seen that portrays
conflict between Indians and people from the East who came into the
American frontier. Why did the settlers move to the West? What
reasons did the Indians have for being angry? Do the students feel
that movie makers are usually fair to both sides in the conflict? Why
or why not?

Objective: To explore events associated with the American West, tell
the class that Paul Goble's *Death of the Iron Horse* is a story about
how a group of young Indian braves tried to keep their land free of
outsiders. As the students listen to the story, ask them to consider if
they think the method of the braves is appropriate.

Guided Activity: Read Goble's book to the class. Ask the students to
suggest reasons why the Indians felt they should stop the Iron Horse
from moving across their land. List the students' responses on the
chalkboard under the title "The Cheyenne Point of View." Do any
students think the owners of the railroad should ask the government
to prosecute the Cheyenne for destruction of property? What might
the owners' reasons be for wanting the braves put on trial? List
responses on the chalkboard under the title "The Railroad Owners'
Point of View."

   Let the students pretend they are running for governor of the
newly formed state of Nebraska. The derailment of the train by the
Cheyenne is a hotly debated issue in the campaign. All candidates for
governor are being asked to tell the voters if they feel the Indians
were right to attack the train, or if they feel the railroad owners are
right to seek prosecution of the Indians. Have the students write a
campaign speech telling which side of the issue they are on and why
they take that stand. Encourage the students to consult the lists on
the chalkboard to get ideas for their speeches.

Extending Activity: Let student volunteers deliver their speeches to
the class. Students may want to dress in costume and decorate the
classroom with campaign posters.

FOLLOW-UP ACTIVITIES FOR TEACHER AND STUDENTS TO SHARE:

1. Read aloud Joan Anderson's *Pioneer Children of Appalachia*. Ask the class to recall the responsibilities assumed by the children. What pleasures did they enjoy? Let the students make corn husk dolls like the children in the book did. To make the dolls, students will need dried corn husks, string, felt-tipped markers, and small pieces of fabric. Have students: (1) Soak the husks in warm water to make them pliable, (2) Fold a large husk in half and tie a piece of string an inch from the fold to make the head, (3) Roll a smaller husk into a stick shape, insert it lengthwise under the string to make the arms, and tie a string at each wrist, (4) Tie another string around the body below the arms, (5) Below the second string, separate the husk into two legs and tie each ankle, and (6) When the dolls are dry, draw a face with the markers and use scraps of fabric to make clothes.

2. Introduce Michael Cooper's *Klondike Fever* by reading the first chapter, "Discovering Gold." Discuss the meaning of the terms "sourdough" and "bonanza." Have the children predict what problems the prospectors will face. Suggest they read the book and complete one of the individual activities for this book.

3. Introduce Russell Freedman's *Buffalo Hunt* by reading the first chapter, "A Gift from the Great Spirit." Let the class discuss how the Indians expressed their respect of the buffalo as a sacred animal. How did the buffalo contribute to the life of the Plains Indians? Share again the George Catlin and Karl Bodmer illustrations found in chapter 1. Read Freedman's note "About the Illustrations" found in the back of the book.

   Tell the class that Olaf Baker's *Where the Buffaloes Begin* (Frederick Warne, 1981) retells a story mentioned in the chapter. Suggest that the students read that book or Paul Goble's *The Great Race of the Birds and Animals* (Bradbury, 1985) which retells the legend Freedman mentioned about the buffaloes eating people. Also, suggest they finish reading *Buffalo Hunt* and complete one of the individual activities for it.

4. Introduce Russell Freedman's *Children of the Wild West* by reading aloud the first chapter, "Frontier Photographers." Show the picture of the pioneer family posing for a photographer in front of their covered wagon. How would a picture of a modern traveling family differ from the one in the book? How would the photographer's equipment be different?

Divide the students into six committees and assign each a chapter to read. Have the groups select several interesting pictures from their chapter. Allow them to pose and photograph modern children in a similar situation. When the photographs are developed, let each committee use their photographs and those in their chapter to illustrate a short presentation that compares the lives of frontier children with the lives of modern children.

5. Introduce Russell Freedman's *Cowboys of the Wild West* by having the class describe what they feel the life of a real cowboy was like in the 1880s. Where did the students get their ideas? Read the first chapter. How was the life of the cowboy described by Freedman different from the students' descriptions? Suggest that those who are interested read the book and do one of the individual activities.

6. Before introducing Russell Freedman's *Indian Chiefs* to the class, prepare a bulletin board with a map of the United States in the middle. Read the introductory chapter, "War Chiefs and Peace Chiefs." Ask students what they think the words "as long as waters run and the grass shall grow" means. Why did the old Kiowa woman say, "We never fully understood that by 'forever' the white man meant 'until we want it for ourselves'"? Reread the last paragraph. Do the students agree or disagree with Chief Joseph's position? Why or why not?

   Ask student volunteers to select one of the chiefs and read the chapter about him. Have each reader select several quotes made by Indians that typify the Indian's view of their relationship with white people. Have the students write the quote with the name and tribe of the Indian being quoted on a piece of brown construction paper cut in the shape of a buffalo hide. Mount the quotations around the map with a piece of yarn stretched from the quotation to the place on the map where the speaker lived. Select a committee to prepare a border for the bulletin board using symbols found in the book's photographs.

7. Before reading Steven Kellogg's *Johnny Appleseed*, have the class share all the facts they know about John Chapman. List their responses on the chalkboard. As they listen to Kellogg's book, ask the class to try to sort out fact from tall tale so they can add to their list of facts. After the book is completed, continue with the students' fact list. Erase any ideas they now decide are fiction. Discuss how the tall tales grew up around Chapman. Suggest that students who wish may go to the school's library media center and find more

information about John Chapman. Have them add any new findings to the list.

8. Over several days read Patricia MacLachlan's *Sarah, Plain and Tall* to the class. Show the students that the book contains no illustrations. Ask the students to consider reasons why the publisher chose to print the book with no pictures. If the students do not suggest that MacLachlan's vivid figurative language makes illustrations unnecessary, perhaps you will suggest the possibility. Ask the students to choose one of the individual activities to complete.

9. Introduce Laura Ingalls Wilder's *On the Banks of Plum Creek* by letting the class suggest ways a pioneer family may have entertained themselves on a cold winter night. Practice ahead of time the slate story Ma told in the chapter called "The Day of Games." Using the blackboard, tell the story to the class. Suggest that the students read the book and complete one of the individual activities.

FOLLOW-UP ACTIVITIES FOR INDIVIDUALS OR SMALL GROUPS:

1. After the teacher has read Joan Anderson's *Pioneer Children of Appalachia*, write a paragraph defending why you would prefer to live in pioneer Appalachia or in your own home today.

2. Read Michael Cooper's *Klondike Fever*. Note the list of food and clothing needed by one person for 18 months, according to the *Seattle Post- Intelligencer*. Check local stores and figure out what that list of items would cost today.

3. Read Michael Cooper's *Klondike Fever*. List the means of travel people used to get to the Klondike. Select one method and write a paragraph describing the problems encountered by people using that mode of transportation.

4. Read Michael Cooper's *Klondike Fever*. Design three advertisements local merchants might have placed in the Dawson newspaper.

5. With a partner read Michael Cooper's *Klondike Fever*. Pretend one of you is a prospector and the other a reporter for the *Seattle Post-Intelligencer*. Let the reporter interview the prospector about the equipment needed to "pan" for gold, how the equipment is used, and what life is like in Dawson.

6. Read Leonard Everett Fisher's *The Alamo*. Write a sentence describing the role of each of the following in the history of the Alamo.

Santa Anna	Jim Bowie
Sam Houston	Davy Crockett
Father Olivares	Susanna Dickinson
William Travis	Clara Driscoll

7. Read Russell Freedman's *Buffalo Hunt*. List the ways Indians used all the parts of the buffalo.

8. Examine the illustrations in Russell Freedman's *Buffalo Hunt*. In the school media center or public library find more information about the life and art of Charles Russell, George Catlin, or one of the other artists whose pictures are included in the book. Share facts about the artist and one of his illustrations from *Buffalo Hunt* with the class.

9. Read Russell Freedman's *Buffalo Hunt*. Write a paragraph describing the reasons the buffalo vanished and the effect that disappearance had on the way of life of the Plains Indians.

10. Read the chapter "Cowboy Clothes and Equipment" in Russell Freedman's *Cowboys of the Wild West*. On a piece of butcher paper draw the various items of clothing and equipment commonly used by cowboys. Label each item. Title your poster with the name of the chapter and mount on the bulletin board.

11. Read the chapter "Ranch Life" in Russell Freedman's *Cowboys of the Wild West*. Write a paragraph comparing ranch life as described by Freedman with that portrayed in a television series such as "Bonanza."

12. Read the chapter "Up the Trail" from Russell Freedman's *Cowboys of the Wild West*. Why did the trail boss insist that cowboys be able to sing? Check with the music teacher or in the media center to see if you can find an old song, such as "Red River Valley," that the cowboys would have sung. Perhaps the music teacher will help the class learn a verse.

13. Read Holling Clancy Holling's *Tree in the Trail*. Make a list of all the events that happened to the tree from the time it was a sapling until the end of the trail.

14. Read Holling Clancy Holling's *Tree in the Trail*. Write a paragraph explaining why the Indians felt the tree was a "Medicine Tree."

15. Read Holling Clancy Holling's *Tree in the Trail*. Write a message that a master of a wagon train may have put in the tree when it served as a post office tree.

16. Read Holling Clancy Holling's *Tree in the Trail*. Reread chapter 16, "A Kansas Twister." On a sheet of paper write a paragraph summarizing the chapter. Check out a book from

the library on tornadoes. Frame your paragraph with drawings and additional facts about tornadoes that Holling could
have used, as he did in chapter 20, "Rendezvous at Council
Grove."

17. Read *Susanna of the Alamo* by John Jakes. Dress up as
    Susanna when she was old and tell the class the story of the
    Alamo massacre of 1836 as Susanna might have told it to
    her grandchildren.

18. Read John Jakes's *Susanna of the Alamo*. Why do you think
    Santa Anna let slaves, women, and children go free? Explain
    the reasons for your opinion in a written paragraph.

19. Read Laurie Lawlor's *Addie across the Prairie*. Organize a
    display of dolls that pioneer children like Addie might have
    had. For the display ask your friends to help you make dolls
    from every day objects like corncobs, corn husks, bones,
    and scraps of cloth. Perhaps a teacher or student who owns
    a china head doll will bring it to display.

20. Read Laurie Lawlor's *Addie across the Prairie*. Using a shoe
    box as the bed of the family's covered wagon, fill it with
    models of the items mentioned in chapter 1 that the Grant
    family took with them on their trip west. Items can be
    made from tooth picks, bits of cloth, small boxes, and salt
    clay. Salt clay can be made using two parts flour and one
    part salt that is mixed and kneaded with enough water for a
    doughlike consistency.

21. Read Meridel Le Sueur's *Little Brother of the Wilderness*.
    Make the scene when Johnny Appleseed meets Abraham
    Lincoln into a play script. With a friend, perform it for the
    class.

22. After hearing Patricia MacLachlan's *Sarah, Plain and Tall*,
    scan the book to find the names of the shells Sarah brought
    from Maine. At the library media center find a picture and
    two facts about each type of shell. Illustrate your list of facts
    with a drawing of each type of shell.

23. After listening to Patricia MacLachlan's *Sarah, Plain and
    Tall*, pick several kinds of wildflowers and dry them the
    way Sarah did. Research the flowers in the media center to
    find their common and scientific names. Mount the dried
    flowers on poster board and label them with each name.

24. After hearing Patricia MacLachlan's *Sarah, Plain and Tall*,
    use colored pencils to make two pictures, one that Sarah
    might have made of Maine, and one she might have made
    of the prairie.

25. After hearing Patricia MacLachlan's *Sarah, Plain and Tall*,
    pretend that both Sarah and Anna kept diaries. Write a

diary entry for each one describing the way she felt about the day Sarah arrived.

26. Read Robert Quackenbush's *Who Let Muddy Boots into the White House?* Pretend that radio was available in Jackson's time. Write a radio news report describing Jackson's inauguration. After sharing it with your teacher, audiotape the report. Share it with the class as time allows.

27. Read Robert Quackenbush's *Who Let Muddy Boots into the White House?* Write a paragraph telling how Jackson got the name "Old Hickory." Draw and caption a cartoon showing Old Hickory running for the presidency.

28. Read *Mr. Yowder and the Windwagon* by Glen Rounds. Go to the library media center and find a tall tale story of Windwagon Smith. List ways in which the two stories are alike.

29. Read *Mr. Yowder and the Windwagon* by Glen Rounds. Create a model of a windwagon. You may want to locate Peggy Parish's book *Let's Be Early Settlers with Daniel Boone* (Harper & Row, 1967) to find directions for making a covered wagon that can be the basis for your new design.

30. Read chapters 1 and 2 in Barbara M. Walker's *The Little House Cookbook.* Write a parargraph describing how the kitchens and ways of preparing food in 1876 when Laura Ingalls Wilder was a child are different from kitchens and food preparation methods of today. Glance through the cookbook and find three recipes you feel would be fun to describe to the class.

31. Select a section from Barbara M. Walker's *The Little House Cookbook.* Read the introduction to the chapter. Skim the recipes in that section and find a simple one, such as "Pancake Men" from "Food from Tilled Fields." Go to the library media center and find the book by Laura Ingalls Wilder in which the recipe you found was mentioned. Read that chapter. Make the recipe at home and bring a sample to school to show or share. Retell the scene from the Wilder book, then describe the recipe.

32. Read Laura Ingalls Wilder's *On the Banks of Plum Creek.* Make a list of all the things Laura, Mary, and Carrie did to have fun. Share your list with the class.

33. Read Laura Ingalls Wilder's *On the Banks of Plum Creek.* As you read the story, make a list of all the foods mentioned in the story such as corn dodgers and biscuits. After making the list, check in Barbara M. Walker's *The Little House Cookbook* to see if you can find recipes for any of the foods on your list. Read facts about the food and how it

was prepared. Make 3" x 5" recipe cards of your favorites. Perhaps you can cook the food for your family.

34. Read Laura Ingalls Wilder's *On the Banks of Plum Creek.* Write a paragraph comparing the way the children celebrated Christmas in the book with the way modern children celebrate the holiday. Using a yard length of heavy thread and a button, make a button string like the one Carrie received at Christmas. Thread the string through the holes in the button and tie the ends of the thread together. Hold the ends of the loop of thread and whirl the button. Alternately pull and release the thread to keep the button spinning.

35. Read Laura Ingalls Wilder's *On the Banks of Plum Creek.* Write a definition of the word "slate" and draw a picture of one. Make a list of all the ways in which Laura and the family used a slate. Ask the library media specialist to help you find a "draw as you tell" story you could share on the chalkboard with the class.

The Civil War Era

STUDENT OBJECTIVES:

1. Discuss the efforts of the abolitionists.
2. Describe the people and events associated with the Civil War.
3. Assess how the Civil War affected peoples' daily lives.
4. Describe the way of life of African-Americans before, during, and after the Civil War.
5. Relate the folklore associated with the Civil War Era.

RECOMMENDED READINGS:

Beatty, Patricia. *Turn Homeward, Hannalee.* William Morrow, 1987.
Two mill worker children from Georgia, forced by the Union army to go north, escape and finally return home. (Objectives 2 and 3)

Ferris, Jeri. *Go Free or Die.* Illustrated by Karen Ritz. Carolrhoda, 1988.
Biography of Harriet Tubman, the former slave who led other slaves to freedom on the Underground Railroad (Objectives 1, 2, 3, and 4)

————. *Walking the Road to Freedom.* Illustrated by Peter E. Hanson. Carolrhoda, 1988.
A woman gains freedom, becomes an orator, speaks out against slavery, and advocates women's rights. (Objectives 1, 2, 3, and 4)

Freedman, Russell. *Lincoln, A Photobiography.* Clarion, 1987.
Portrays the life of the Civil War president, using text and photographs. (Objectives 2, 3, and 4)

Fritz, Jean. *Stonewall.* Illustrated by Stephen Gammell. G. P. Putnam's, 1979.
Relates the boyhood life of Thomas Jackson and his role in the Civil War. (Objectives 2 and 3)

Hamilton, Virginia. *The People Could Fly.* Illustrated by Leo and Diane Dillon. Alfred A. Knopf, 1985.
A collection of African-American folktales about animals, the supernatural, and striving for freedom. (Objectives 4 and 5)

Harris, Joel Chandler. *Jump Again!* Adapted by Van Dyke Parks. Illustrated by Barry Moser. Harcourt Brace Jovanovich, 1987.
Presents five Brer Rabbit tales in simplified dialect. (Objective 5)

Johnson, Neil. *The Battle of Gettysburg.* Four Winds, 1989.
Using photographs from the 125th anniversary reenactment, the famous Civil War battle is described. (Objective 2)

Lester, Julius. *The Tales of Uncle Remus.* Illustrated by Jerry Pinkney. Dial, 1987.
Includes the tales of Brer Rabbit and the animals he tricked. (Objective 5)

————. *To Be a Slave.* Illustrated by Tom Feelings. Dial, 1968.
A collection of narratives taken from interviews with former slaves. (Objectives 1 and 4)

Nixon, Joan Lowery. *A Family Apart.* Bantam, 1987.
During the Civil War period, six siblings whose mother is unable to support them are adopted into midwest farm families. (Objectives 1, 3, and 4)

Reit, Seymour. *Behind Rebel Lines.* Harcourt Brace Jovanovich, 1988.
Describes how Emma Edmonds enlisted in the Union army and served as a spy. (Objectives 2 and 3)

Sanfield, Steve. *The Adventures of High John the Conqueror.* Illustrated by John Ward. Orchard, 1989.
Stories about the African-American trickster hero who outwitted his masters and other white men after freedom came. (Objectives 4 and 5)

Turner, Ann. *Nettie's Trip South.* Illustrated by Ronald Himler. Macmillan, 1987.
A 10-year-old girl travels from New York to Richmond before the Civil War and is shocked by the aspects of slavery she encounters. (Objectives 1 and 4)

GROUP INTRODUCTORY ACTIVITY:

Preparation: Locate Ann Turner's *Nettie's Trip South*. Collect a large piece of butcher paper and supplies for making a mural.

Focus: Ask the students to discuss what they know about the life of a slave in the South in the days before the Civil War. What jobs did slaves do? Under what conditions did they live?

Objective: To assist in describing the way of life of African-Americans before the Civil War, introduce Ann Turner's *Nettie's Trip South*. Read aloud the note on the back of the Title Page which tells that the story is based on the author's great-grandmother's diary describing how a trip she made from her home in the North to visit the South compelled her to become a committed abolitionist. Discuss the meaning of "abolitionist." Ask the students to listen for reasons why Nettie became an abolitionist.

Guided Activity: After reading Turner's book to the class, ask them to discuss what caused Nettie's intense reaction to slavery. How did her own comfortable life increase her feelings of sympathy and horror?

Tell the class that artists and writers often use their creative talents to protest unfairness in society. Let the students pretend they are abolitionist artists who wish to protest slavery by creating a mural of the hardships of life as a slave. Divide the class into committees. Let each committee select one of Ronald Himler's illustrations in *Nettie's Trip South* to use as a guide in developing a section of the mural.

Extending Activity: Let a committee of students search the media center's catalog for books about slavery. Ask the library media specialist if the class can display the mural and books about slavery in the media center during Black History Month.

FOLLOW-UP ACTIVITIES FOR TEACHER AND STUDENTS TO SHARE:

1. Read the author's note as a way to introduce Jeri Ferris's *Walking the Road to Freedom*. Tell the students Sojourner Truth played many roles in her lifetime, and they will be discussing those roles over the next few days as you read the book aloud.

    Read chapter 1. Write the name "Sojourner Truth" in a circle drawn in the middle of a piece of butcher paper. Ask the students to suggest a word or short phrase that identifies Sojourner in her early life. Let the class select the one or two best ideas, perhaps "slave" and "Isabelle." Using a webbing technique, write the selected words in circles drawn at the end of lines that extend from the central circle.

Read chapter 2. Let the class decide what new roles Sojourner now plays, e. g., "mother" or "free-woman." Add these to the web. Continue reading and webbing the roles Sojourner played in the society. After chapter 3, students might select the roles of "orator," "abolitionist," or "women's rights advocate." After chapters 4 and 5, they could choose "teacher," "nurse," or "civil rights advocate."

2. Ask the students to tell what they know about Abraham Lincoln. Read the first chapter "The Mysterious Mr. Lincoln" in Russell Freedman's *Lincoln, A Photobiography*. Let students share what new ideas they learned about Lincoln.

    Ask a committee of six interested students to read the book and develop a board game that identifies important aspects of Lincoln's life. Assign each committee member one of the remaining chapters to read. Suggest that each reader select five interesting facts from his or her chapter and write each fact on an index card. The students may use the cards to develop the game.

3. Introduce Virginia Hamilton's *The People Could Fly* by reading her introduction about African-American folktales and their creation. Then read to the class the story "Carrying the Running-Aways" and Hamilton's note following the story. Let the class discuss why they think Hamilton included this underground railroad story in the collection. Suggest to the class that they do one of the individual activities suggested for this book.

4. Before reading Julius Lester's *The Tales of Uncle Remus*, ask the class if they have ever heard of Brer Rabbit. If so, where did they hear of him? Tell the class that the most often told story of Brer Rabbit is "Brer Rabbit and the Tar Baby." Read that story to the class. Tell the class that this story is an adaptation of "Wakaima and the Clay Man," a story brought from the west coast of Africa by people who were brought to America as slaves. Show the children Van Dyke Park's adaptation of Joel Chandler Harris's *Jump Again!* and Virginia Hamilton's *The People Could Fly*. Tell students they contain other versions of the tar baby story. Encourage students to do the individual activity listed for *Jump Again!*

5. Introduce Julius Lester's *To Be a Slave* as a collection of interviews with ex-slaves. Tell students information from the author's note about how these personal stories were collected. Read the introductory quotation about the exclusion of African-Americans from American history books. Select several of the narratives to read to the class. Show

students one of the pages and explain that the italicized paragraphs are Lester's comments. The ones collected from the slaves are in standard type. Ask the students to scan the book and find a narrative that interests them to read aloud to the class.

6. Introduce Seymour Reit's *Behind Rebel Lines* by reading the introductory quote from Emma's memoirs and the two-page Introduction "To Begin." Let the class discuss the meaning of the quote, "Through our great good fortune, in our youth our hearts were touched with fire." Ask the class to anticipate what wild adventures the introduction may be referring to. Ask for a volunteer to read the book and share Emma's problems and accomplishments. Did any of the class's suggested adventures actually happen?

7. Introduce Steve Sanfield's *The Adventures of High John the Conqueror* by reading the Introduction and the first tale. Let the class discuss how the stories of High John the Conqueror must have made the slaves feel? What do the students think the title means? Have the students characterize High John. Assign individual stories to student volunteers to read independently. Have them describe High John's trick on a 5" × 7" index card. The card can be decorated with a border based on a motif in the story. Place on a bulletin board titled "High John's Tricks."

FOLLOW-UP ACTIVITIES FOR INDIVIDUALS OR SMALL GROUPS:

1. Read Patricia Beatty's *Turn Homeward, Hannalee*. List five ideas or events you learned about the Civil War period by reading this book.

2. Read Patricia Beatty's *Turn Homeward, Hannalee*. Write a conversation in which Hannalee tells her mother about her journey back home to Georgia. Have Hannalee explain why the decision to return was such a difficult one, and have her describe the most dangerous situations she encountered on the way.

3. Read Patricia Beatty's *Turn Homeward, Hannalee*. Although the characters are fictional, much of the story is based on facts. Did reading the book change your feelings about how the Civil War affected ordinary people? If so, in what way? If not, what ideas you had about the war were reinforced by reading the story? Write your thoughts in a paragraph.

4. Read *Go Free or Die*, a biography of Harriet Tubman written by Jeri Ferris. Pretend you are a newspaper reporter

in 1913 who will be allowed to interview 93-year-old Harriet Tubman. You have been told she has only enough strength to answer three questions. Make a list of the three questions you would ask.

5. Read Jeri Ferris's *Go Free or Die*, a biography of Harriet Tubman. When you finish reading, go back through the book and study Karen Ritz's illustrations. Decide what aspect of Harriet's life each illustration is depicting and write a caption for each one.

6. Read Jeri Ferris's *Go Free or Die*, a biography of Harriet Tubman. Write a paragraph describing two ways the song "Go Down Moses" was important to Harriet's life. Show your paragraph to the music teacher. Ask him or her to help you find a recording of the song and any other spirituals about freedom. Set up a Harriet Tubman listening center in your classroom.

7. Read Jean Fritz's *Stonewall*. Write a title for each of the chapters. Have your titles give clues of what will happen in the chapter.

8. Read Jean Fritz's *Stonewall*. List five battles in which Stonewall's troops played an important role and write a brief paragraph describing each.

9. Read Jean Fritz's *Stonewall*. Write a paragraph describing why veterans of Stonewall's brigade "wanted to sleep with the Old Man just once more."

10. As you read Jean Fritz's *Stonewall* examine Gammell's illustrations. List five other scenes you wish Gammell would have illustrated. Briefly describe what you would want included in each picture.

11. Read "Papa John's Tall Tale" from Virginia Hamilton's *The People Could Fly*. Make a list of the exaggerations in the story.

12. Read "How Nehemiah Got Free" and Virginia Hamilton's note following the story in *The People Could Fly*. Explain to the class the meaning and significance of Juneteenth.

13. Read "He Lion, Bruh Bear, and Bruh Rabbit" from Virginia Hamilton's *The People Could Fly*. Write a short paragraph summarizing the plot of the story and explaining why man was chosen as the one to fear.

14. Read Neil Johnson's *The Battle of Gettysburg*. Pretend you are a soldier who was wounded in the battle and hospitalized. From your hospital bed, write a letter home describing the battle. Use names of generals and specific places in your description.

15. After being introduced to Julius Lester's *The Tales of Uncle Remus*, read "The Talking House." Rewrite the story into a play script with three characters: a narrator, Brer Rabbit, and Brer Wolf. With two friends, read the play for the class.

16. Read Joan Lowery Nixon's *A Family Apart*. Pretend you are Frances writing a letter to her mother in New York City. Describe your experiences as a "conductor" on the Underground Railroad.

17. After the teacher shares "Brer Rabbit and the Tar Baby" in Julius Lester's *The Tales of Uncle Remus*, read "The Wonderful Tar-Baby Story" in Van Dyke Parks's adaptation of Joel Chandler Harris's *Jump Again!* and "Doc Rabbit, Bruh Fox, and Tar Baby" in Virginia Hamilton's *The People Could Fly*. Make a list of the differences in the three versions.

America, Land of Change

STUDENT OBJECTIVES:

1. Discuss the contributions of immigrants and the problems associated with immigration.
2. Explain how economic and environmental conditions have influenced the lives of late nineteenth and twentieth century Americans.
3. Describe efforts to establish and preserve the rights and traditions of minority groups.
4. Analyze how Americans responded to war in the twentieth century.

RECOMMENDED READINGS:

Adoff, Arnold, ed. *My Black Me*. E. P. Dutton, 1974.
A collection of poems by 26 African-American poets. (Objective 3)

Altman, Susan. *Extraordinary Black Americans from Colonial to Contemporary Times*. Children's Press, 1989.
Short biographies of African-Americans identify their personal achievements and how they worked to establish and preserve civil rights. (Objective 3)

Ancona, George. *The American Family Farm.* Text by Joan Anderson. Harcourt Brace Jovanovich, 1989.
A photo-essay about how three farm families have overcome adversity and continue to have faith in their way of life. (Objective 2)

Avi. *Shadrach's Crossing.* Pantheon, 1983.
In 1932 island villagers, suffering from the Depression, allow liquor smugglers to terrorize them until a boy determines to seek justice. (Objective 2)

Boyd, Candy Dawson. *Charlie Pippin.* Macmillan, 1987.
Eleven-year-old Charlie researches the Vietnam War and reaches a new understanding of her father's bitterness. (Objectives 3 and 4)

Bunting, Eve. *How Many Days to America?* Illustrated by Beth Peck. Clarion, 1988.
After a dangerous boat trip, refugees from a Caribbean island arrive in America on Thanksgiving Day. (Objective 1)

Cobblestone. Vol. 10, No. 7. (July 1989) Entire issue.
A thematic issue devoted to the Navajo Nation: their homes, folklore, customs, art, and contribution in World War II. (Objectives 2, 3, and 4)

De Jong, Meindert. *The House of Sixty Fathers.* Illustrated by Maurice Sendak. Harper & Row, 1956.
Tien Pao, a small Chinese boy, is rescued by American soldiers in the early days of the Japanese invasion of China. (Objective 4)

Devaney, John. *Franklin Delano Roosevelt, President.* Walker, 1987.
A biography of the president who led the nation through the Great Depression and World War II. (Objectives 2 and 4)

Fisher, Leonard Everett. *Ellis Island.* Holiday House, 1986.
Presents the story of immigrants arriving at Ellis Island from 1897 to 1932. (Objective 1)

Lewis, Claudia. *Long Ago in Oregon.* Illustrated by Joel Fontaine. Harper & Row, 1987.
Through poetry, the life of a girl in 1917 in an Oregon small town is shared. (Objective 4)

Meltzer, Milton. *Mary McLeod Bethune.* Illustrated by Stephen Marchesi. Viking, 1987.
A biography of a leader who deserved the title "Voice of Black Hope." (Objective 3)

Mendez, Phil. *The Black Snowman.* Illustrated by Carole Byard. Scholastic, 1989.
When a magic kente brings a black snowman to life, Jacob learns to be proud of himself and his African-American heritage. (Objective 3)

Mitchell, Barbara. *We'll Race You, Henry.* Illustrated by Kathy Haubrich. Carolrhoda, 1986.
Describes the efforts of the developer of the Model T. (Objective 2)

Quackenbush, Robert. *Don't You Dare Shoot that Bear!* Prentice-Hall, 1984.
Cartoon illustrations add humor to the biography of the 26th president whose conservation efforts are evident today. (Objective 2)

Schroeder, Alan. *Ragtime Tumpie.* Illustrated by Bernie Fuchs. Little, Brown, 1989.
Describes Josephine Baker's childhood dreams of becoming a dancer despite the poverty she encountered in St. Louis in the early 1900s. (Objective 2)

Schwartz, Alvin. *When I Grew Up Long Ago.* Illustrated by Harold Berson. J. B. Lippincott, 1978.
Brief descriptions of childhood activities across the United States from 1890–1940. (Objectives 1, 2, and 4)

Sneve, Virginia Driving Hawk. *Dancing Teepees.* Illustrated by Stephen Gammell. Holiday House, 1989.
Presents traditional and contemporary Native American poetry. (Objective 3)

Taylor, Mildred. *The Gold Cadillac.* Illustrated by Michael Hays. Dial, 1987.
In 1950, an African-American family living in Toledo drive their new Cadillac to Mississippi but leave it in Memphis because of harassment by white police in the South. (Objective 3)

Uchida, Yoshiko. *Journey to Topaz.* Rev. ed. Illustrated by Donald Carrick. Creative Arts, 1985.
Describes the hardship of a Japanese-American family forced to leave their home and be imprisoned unjustly during World War II. (Objectives 3 and 4)

GROUP INTRODUCTORY ACTIVITY:

Preparation: Locate *When I Grew Up Long Ago* by Alvin Schwartz.

Focus: Share with the students a personal family story that your parents or grandparents told you about life when they "grew up long ago." Invite the students to share a family story they heard from their parents or grandparents. After all volunteers have shared, tell students that today families often live far away from their relatives, and these stories can be a treasured way to remember them.

Objective: To introduce the concept of how economic and environmental conditions have influenced the lives of late nineteenth and twentieth century Americans, share Alvin Schwartz's *When I Grew Up Long Ago.* Tell the children the book is a collection of brief stories that reveal life in times past.

Guided Activity: Read aloud Schwartz's Introduction, "A Vanished World," and the first entries in "What We Wore," "How We Got Around," "After Supper," "Strangers," and "Two Wars." Let the class compare and contrast life then and now.

Assign each student one section of the book to read. Ask each to select a favorite entry from the section to read to the class. The student sharing "Games We Played" may want to demonstrate the one chosen. Perhaps the class can learn to sing the song chosen from "Songs We Sang."

After all have selected a story to share, have a "Turn of the Century" party. Perhaps the students would like to invite their parents or another class. Let each student present their selection from the book. Ask a volunteer parent to use the "Oatmeal Cookies" recipe to make refreshments for the party.

Extending Activity: Have each student write one or more "When I Grew Up" stories about their own lives. Arrange their stories by categories similar to those used by Alvin Schwartz in *When I Grew Up Long Ago*. Bind the stories into a class book. Ask the media specialist to keep the book in the school's library for future students to read.

FOLLOW-UP ACTIVITIES FOR TEACHER AND STUDENTS TO SHARE:

1. Introduce Arnold Adoff's *My Black Me* by telling the children that this is a collection of poems by African-American poets. Let the class suggest what the topics of the poems might be. Read "Death of Dr. King #1" and "Harriet Tubman." Let the students discuss King's and Tubman's contributions to the lives of black Americans. Read "My People." What is Langston Hughes saying in this poem? Read Don Lee's "From Blackwoman Poems." Let the students talk about the meaning of each line. Read William Harris's "A Grandfather Poem." Have the children discuss the meaning of the word "dignity." Suggest that each child use either Lee's or Harris's poem as a pattern to write a poem about his or her own mother, grandfather, or special relative.

2. Introduce Susan Altman's *Extraordinary Black Americans from Colonial to Contemporary Times* by reading the short biographies of Mary McLeod Bethune and W. E. B. Du Bois. Let the class discuss the contributions of each. Ask each class member to read one two-page biography and share with the class that person's contribution to American life.

3. Introduce George Ancona's *The American Family Farm* by reading the Introduction and the Afterword. Based on the facts presented, let the class discuss what the three farm families appear to have in common. Ask for three volunteers to read and report on the life of one of the three families shared in the book. After the reports, have the class continue their discussion about common farm problems and the role of the family farm in American life.

If proximity allows, have a local farmer visit the class and describe the problems and satisfactions of farm life. If the farmer lived on the farm as a child, ask about changes in the way the farm is managed that are due to technology. Ask how the farmer was affected by the drought of 1988.

4. Before reading Eve Buntings *How Many Days to America?* explain to the class that the book is about refugees that recently came to America from the Caribbean. Ask them to recall why the original Pilgrims came to America and the problems they encountered. As the book is read, students should think of comparisons between the two groups. After the story is completed, let the class compare the Pilgrims and present day refugees described in the book. Guide students to explore the facts that on both voyages people got sick, they ran out of food and drink, they did not know where they would land, and both groups felt the need for thanksgiving.

5. Introduce *Cobblestone* by reading "Navajo Code Talkers," pp. 33–35. Discuss the importance of the role the Navajo played in World War II. What various occupations did the Navajo code talkers assume after the war? Using an overhead projector, share the talkers cryptogram on page 39 with the class. Tell them that "A" is "d," "K" is "t," "L" is "h," and "M" is "e." Ask them to copy the cryptogram and see if anyone can figure out the first sentence before the next class period. Tell the class that the cryptogram relates to the article they have just heard and discussed.

   Tell the class that as soon as someone has figured out the cryptogram, the *Cobblestone* magazine will be on the reading table. Ask each child to read one article and do a suggested activity as an individual or in pairs.

6. Introduce Claudia Lewis's *Long Ago in Oregon* by asking if anyone has any idea of what might be important in the life of a young girl in Oregon in 1917–1918. Read the first poem. Does anyone know an important historical event that happened in 1917? Read "Over There." Discuss what children did to help out during World War I. If there were a war now, do the students suppose children would be knitting squares for blankets? What might today's children be doing in response to war?

   Read "Christmas Trees." Let children identify the details that made them know the poem is about a time long ago. If the class were going to write a book of poems that revealed life in today's world, what topics would they choose? List the topics on the board as suggestions are given. Ask each member of the class to select a topic and write a short poem about it. Notice that Lewis's poems were written with no rhyme.

7. Read *The Black Snowman* by Phil Mendez aloud to the class. After reading the book, ask the students why Jacob said he hated being black in the beginning of the story. What happened to cause him to feel differently about his African ancestry? Do the students know from what country or continent their ancestors came? Have them go home and ask parents or grandparents to tell them about their ancestry and at least one reason why they should feel proud of their heritage. Let them share their family discussions with the class.

8. Read aloud the Introduction to Virginia Sneve's *Dancing Teepees*. Ask the students to recall any lullabies their mothers or other adults sing to children. Have them repeat the lines of any they remember. Read "Coo...Ah...Coo," the Paiute cradle song. What phrases in this lullaby would soothe a baby to sleep? Read "I Watched an Eagle Soar." What does the last line mean? Read "The Black Turkey-Gobbler." What is the Mescalero Apache describing? How might we describe the sunrise?

   Prepare a transparency with the poem "I Rise, I Rise" on it. Tell the children they will be reading chorally an Osage prayer that is said before a young man's first buffalo hunt. Have them solemnly read, "I rise, I rise," as a chorus for the intervening lines.

9. Read Mildred Taylor's *The Gold Cadillac* to the class. Why did the family take food with them on the trip? Let the class discuss the racial signs encountered by the family in the South. What problems did the family face? Why did they go back to Memphis and leave the Cadillac there? Ask a committee to research what changes have occurred to lessen racial injustice in the past 40 years and to report their findings to the class.

10. Introduce Yoshiko Uchida's *Journey to Topaz* by reading the author's Prologue and the first chapter. Urge one or more children to read the book so they can share with the class what happened to Yuki.

    After the readers have shared the book, ask a volunteer to research in the library media center or public library to find out what the United States government did in the 1980s to try to repay the Japanese-American families for the injustice they suffered. After the reports are given, let the students discuss how they would feel if their family were treated as Yuki's was. Could later action by the government truly repay them?

FOLLOW-UP ACTIVITIES FOR INDIVIDUALS OR SMALL GROUPS:

1. Look at the list of poets whose works are included in Arnold Adoff's *My Black Me*. Check in the library to see if you can find other poems by Lucille Clifton, Langston Hughes, or one of the other poets mentioned. Select a favorite poem and share it with the class.

2. Read Avi's *Shadrach's Crossing*. If you were writing the ending of the book, would it have been the one chosen by Avi? If so, justify Avi's choice. If not, outline the ending you would have chosen.

3. Read Avi's *Shadrach's Crossing*. The island families allowed the smugglers to terrorize them because of their hopelessness caused by the Depression. Find a factual book in the library media center or the public library about the Depression. List and briefly describe five problems caused by the Depression.

4. Read Candy Boyd's *Charlie Pippin*. Research facts about nuclear war and facts about the Vietnam War that would fit into Charlie's "A New Way of Thinking" speech at the point where she dropped the index cards. Complete her speech as you think it might have been written. Read Charlie's speech and your addition to the class.

5. Read Candy Boyd's *Charlie Pippin*. Why did Charlie's father refuse to share his war experiences? Interview a Vietnam veteran in your community to find out that person's attitude about the war. Report your findings to the class.

6. Read "Dine, The People of the Navajo Nation," pp 4–5, in *Cobblestone*, July 1989. List three new words and their meanings that you found in the article.

7. Read "At Home with Willie Peshlakai," pp 6–10, in *Cobblestone*, July 1989. Write a paragraph Willie Peshlakai might have written to describe his home.

8. Read "Navajoland," pp 11–13, in *Cobblestone*, July 1989. Go to the library media center and find information about Canyon de Chelly. Bring back a picture or information to share with the class to show why they might like to visit there.

9. Read "Build a Navajo Hogan," pp 23–26, in *Cobblestone*, July 1989. Follow the directions and make a hogan.

10. Read "A Voice for Her People," pp 36–38 in *Cobblestone*, July 1989. Write a paragraph about Annie Wauneka that could have been used an an introduction when she was awarded the Medal of Honor by the Navajo Nation.

11. Read Meindert De Jong's *The House of Sixty Fathers*. Do you feel the ending was realistic? Why or why not? Write a different ending De Jong might have chosen.

12. Read John Devaney's *Franklin Delano Roosevelt, President*. Make a list of what you feel are the most interesting things about F. D. R. and his greatest accomplishments during his presidency. Interview two senior citizens who remember when Roosevelt was elected president in 1932. See what they remember about Roosevelt and his years in the White House. Compare their memories with the items on your list. What did they remember about Roosevelt, the man? Share your findings with the class.

13. Read Leonard Fisher's *Ellis Island*. Pretend you arrived in the United States as an immigrant and were processed through Ellis Island. Write a letter to a friend in the country from which you came describing your arrival at Ellis Island and how you felt as you went through the immigration procedures.

14. Read Milton Meltzer's *Mary McLeod Bethune*. Make a large poster titled "Mary McLeod Bethune: Voice of Black Hope." Draw symbols such as a book, a train, a school-house, etc., that identifies her lifetime accomplishments. Add one sentence to describe each symbol. Post on the bulletin board for the class to share.

15. Read Barbara Mitchell's *We'll Race You, Henry*. Draw a picture of the Model T and write a brief paragraph describing it. Label the picture with the sale price in 1914. Draw a picture of a new car of your choice. Write a brief description and label it with the current price.

16. Read Robert Quackenbush's *Don't You Dare Shoot That Bear!* Using teddy bear characters, make a newspaper comic strip that shows Theodore Roosevelt, an early twentieth century president, making lasting contributions to conservation.

17. Read Alan Schroeder's *Ragtime Tumpie*. Write a paragraph describing how Tumpie stuck to her dream of becoming a dancer. Write a second paragraph discussing what you can do now to prepare for the job you want to pursue as an adult?

The United States Today and Tomorrow

STUDENT OBJECTIVES:

1. Examine life in America today and consider what the future may hold.
2. Identify how technology, modern communications, and space exploration have affected present day America and speculate about future technological advancements.
3. Discuss the relationship among states of the United States and among the countries of the world.
4. Consider the involvement of a variety of cultures evidenced in the humor and folklore that is part of the American tradition.

RECOMMENDED READINGS:

Ashabranner, Brent. *To Live in Two Worlds.* Illustrated by Paul Conklin. Dodd, Mead, 1984.
Introduces American Indian children from many tribes, sharing their educational problems and successes. (Objective 1)

Berliner, Don. *Airplanes of the Future.* Lerner, 1987.
Describes designs for the future that will make personal planes, airliners, and military aircraft more efficient. (Objectives 1 and 2)

The Diane Goode Book of American Folk Tales & Songs. Collected by Ann Durell. E. P. Dutton, 1989.
Selected folktales and songs represent America's cultural and regional diversity. (Objective 4)

Mayers, Florence Cassen. *The National Air Space Museum ABC.* Harry N. Abrams, 1987.
The letters of the alphabet are the framework for a brief illustrated history of aviation and space technology. (Objectives 1 and 2)

Parker, Nancy Winslow. *The President's Car.* Thomas Y. Crowell, 1981.
Illustrations and brief text identify the presidential vehicles from Washington to Reagan. (Objectives 1 and 2)

Pringle, Laurence. *Living in a Risky World.* William Morrow, 1989.
Identifies the hazards of modern life and describes strategies for managing and reducing them. (Objectives 1 and 2)

San Souci, Robert D. *The Boy and the Ghost.* Illustrated by J. Brian Pinkney. Simon and Schuster, 1989.
An African-American boy spends a night in a haunted house in order to bring a treasure to his family. (Objective 4)

Schwartz, Alvin. *Cross Your Fingers, Spit in Your Hat.* Illustrated by Glen Rounds. J. B. Lippincott, 1974.
Superstitions are organized by topic and the sources of superstition throughout the United States are identified. (Objective 4)

Siebert, Diane. *Heartland.* Illustrated by Wendell Minor. Thomas Y. Crowell, 1989.
The spirit of the Midwest is evoked through poetic text and striking illustrations. (Objective 1)

Thompson, Kathleen. *Alaska.* Raintree, 1988.
Photographs enhance the brief text describing the people, the history, and the future of the 49th state. (Objectives 1 and 2)

West, Robin. *Far Out!* Illustrated by Bob Wolfe, Diane Wolfe, and Priscilla Kiedrowski. Carolrhoda, 1987.
Household items provide materials for constructing a supersonic space patroller, lunar colony, and other futuristic models. (Objectives 1 and 2)

Williams, Vera B. and Williams, Jennifer. *Stringbean's Trip to the Shining Sea.* Greenwillow, 1988.
Stringbean sends postcards each day describing his trip to the Pacific Ocean. (Objective 3)

Woods, Harold and Woods, Geraldine. *The United Nations.* Franklin Watts, 1985.
Describes the organization and specialized agencies of the United Nations. (Objective 3)

GROUP INTRODUCTORY ACTIVITY:

Preparation: Locate *The National Air and Space Museum ABC* by Florence Cassen Mayers.

Focus: Challenge the students to think of at least one term about aviation and space for every letter of the alphabet. Suggest they consider vehicles, people, events, and places that have played a part in air and space exploration from its beginning to now. List their suggestions on the chalkboard in alphabetical order. If students are unable to find terms for each letter, appoint a committee of students to search in the library media center for possibilities.

Objective: The group introductory activity addresses the objective of identifying how technology, modern communications, and space exploration have affected present day America, motivating students to speculate about future advancements.

Guided Activity: Tell the students that air and space exploration has been a major focus of our society during the twentieth century, and it promises to play a role in the twenty-first century also. Have the students research an item from the alphabetical list on the chalkboard. If necessary, ask interested students to select a second item so that all letters of the alphabet are represented. Direct each student to illustrate and write a paragraph about his or her selected topic. Combine the work into a class air and space alphabet book.

When the class has completed the book, read Florence Cassen Mayers's *The National Air and Space Museum ABC*. Let the students compare their book to the one by Mayers. In which instances do they prefer the choices the class made for inclusion in their book? Why? What items does the Mayers book include that the class did not consider?

Extending Activity: Encourage the students to think about advancements that might be made in air and space exploration in the next century. Challenge them to use their imaginations to create a second air and space alphabet book that might be made by students 100 years from now.

FOLLOW-UP ACTIVITIES FOR TEACHER AND STUDENTS TO SHARE:

1. Introduce Brent Ashabranner's *To Live in Two Worlds* by reading chapter 1, "Our Youth Are Our Future." Let the class discuss the educational problems faced by Native Americans. What hopes do they have for the future? Tell the students that within each chapter of the book a young person is introduced. Assign the chapters to volunteers to read. After reading the chapter, each should write a short speech titled "My Story." Direct students to write in first person as if the student were the Native American described in the book. Let the students give their speeches to the class.

2. Introduce *The Diane Goode Book of American Folk Tales and Songs* by telling the simple, humorous story, "The Twist-Mouth Family," a New England folktale. Suggest to the class that they ask their parents what section of America or from what ethnic background their great-grandparents came. After each child finds out this information, ask them to check to see if Diane Goode has illustrated a folktale appropriate for their family. If so, read the story and prepare a 3" × 5" index card with the name of the story, the title of the book, and a short one paragraph annotation describing the content of the story. If students find no appropriate story in this collection, suggest they ask the school library media specialist or public librarian to help

them locate a folktale to read and annotate. Post the cards on a small bulletin board titled "Bibliography of Stories from Our Heritage."

3. Introduce Laurence Pringle's *Living in a Risky World* by having the class list the hazards they feel are part of modern life. Read the Introduction. See if the class can now add to the list. Explain that the book is concerned with risk identification, management, and control.

   Ask each of a committee of six to read an assigned chapter so they can present a panel discussion for the class focused on the areas of risk, identification, and control. After the discussion, other members of the class may want to write to a government agency or public interest organization listed in the back of the book, requesting information about the reduction of hazards. After sharing important points with the class, the material may be given to the library media center to be added to the vertical file.

4. Before introducing Alvin Schwartz's *Cross Your Fingers, Spit in Your Hat*, scan the Source List at the back of the book to find superstitions which list your state as a source and ones which you feel the class would particularly enjoy. Write the terms "folk belief," "superstition," "charm," "amulet," "talisman," and "taboo" on the chalkboard. Discuss the meaning of the words, using the notes at the end of the book as a source. Ask the students to tell any superstitions they know. List them on a page of butcher paper. Read selected superstitions from Schwartz's book to the class.

   Ask the students each to choose a superstition not illustrated by Glen Rounds, copy it at the bottom of a sheet of paper, illustrate it, and share it with the class.

   Have the students ask adult family members to recall any superstitions they remember from childhood. Let the students add these to the butcher paper list.

5. Have the class read Diane Siebert's *Heartland* as a choral. Let the class as a whole say, "I am the Heartland," when signalled to do so. Assign a different student to read each page. After the poem is read, let the class discuss the future of the small farmer. What threatens the family farm? If the students live in an area not concerned with agricultural affairs, research may be needed before this book is presented and the discussion held. If needed, appoint a committee to research and report to the class. Suggest that students do the individual activity suggested for this book.

6. Unless Alaska is the home state of the students, read aloud Kathleen Thompson's *Alaska*. Discuss why the state's nick-

name is "The Last Frontier." Let the class identify current problems faced by the state. If any member of the community has lived in or traveled in Alaska, ask that person to share pictures and impressions of the state. Encourage students to do the individual activity suggested for this book.

7. To introduce *The United Nations* by Harold and Geraldine Woods, read the short section (pp. 14-18) on the organization of the United Nations and the General Assembly. Let the class discuss the reason such an organization is necessary. Why is it difficult for such a large organization to accomplish its goals? Divide the class into small committees. Assign each group one of the other five United Nations divisions or a special agency. Ask each committee to read the short section in the Woods' book about the topic and research in the library media center for more information about the accomplishments and problems of the assigned division or agency. Let the committees report their findings to the class.

FOLLOW-UP ACTIVITIES FOR INDIVIDUALS OR SMALL GROUPS:

1. Read the chapter "Personal Airplanes" in Don Berliner's *Airplanes of the Future*. As a reporter, write a news article describing the futuristic aviation ideas people will be interested in reading.

2. Read the chapter "Airliners of the Future" in Don Berliner's *Airplanes of the Future*. Pretend you are a pilot. Have a friend interview you about what people can expect in future airplane trips. Share the interview with the class.

3. Read the chapter "Military Aircraft" in Don Berliner's *Airplanes of the Future*. Pretend you are the Secretary of Defense. Describe specific advanced ideas found in Berliner's book that might influence Congress to allocate money to the defense budget. Give your talk to the class as if they were the Congress.

4. Read Nancy Winslow Parker's *The President's Car*. List the differences in a presidential motorcade in Calvin Coolidge's administration and that of Jimmy Carter 50 years later. What are the reasons for these differences?

5. Read Nancy Winslow Parker's *The President's Car*. List the security features you predict will be evident in a presidential car in 2010.

6. Read Robert D. San Souci's *The Boy and the Ghost*. Write a paragraph describing the character traits in the boy that caused him to succeed when so many others failed.

7. Read Robert D. San Souci's *The Boy and the Ghost*. Read the note at the end telling the reader the origin of the story. Write a paragraph telling why you think this story survived and became a part of African-American folk literature.

8. Read Robert D. San Souci's *The Boy and the Ghost*. Read the note at the end telling the reader the origin of the story. Check with your school media center or public library and see if you can find Sibyl Hancock's *Esteban and the Ghost* (Dial, 1983) or any other version of the story. Write in a paragraph your thoughts about why there are so many versions of this story.

9. After the class has shared Diane Siebert's *Heartland*, examine the illustration which shows land in the foreground and the city in the background. Consider the way cities grow and write what the land might say 20 years from now.

10. After Kathleen Thompson's *Alaska* has been read aloud in class, review the book by examining the illustrations. Check with an airline company or travel agency to find how much it would cost to fly from your city to Juneau, Alaska. Using Thompson's book and other sources in the library media center, make a list of sights you would like to see in Alaska and describe how you would travel to each from Juneau.

11. Examine Robin West's *Far Out!* Select and create an item and write a paragraph describing its use in the world of the future.

12. Read *Stringbean's Trip to the Shining Sea* by Vera and Jennifer Williams. For this activity you will need an outline map of the United States. Perhaps your teacher can provide one, or you can trace one from a source in the library media center.

    Stringbean sent one card each day after leaving Kansas. How long did it take for him to reach the Pacific Ocean? Using any clues found on the cards, draw on the map what you feel was the route Stringbean took. Write a paragraph telling why you decided on that route.

13. Read *Stringbean's Trip to the Shining Sea* by Vera and Jennifer Williams. Stringbean says he still has four oceans he has never seen. From his home in Kansas, plan his trip to an ocean other than the Pacific. Decide what route he will take, what kinds of transportation he will use, how long the trip will take, and what sights he will see along the way. Write at least one postcard he would have mailed along the

way. Include some of the information you decided upon while planning the trip. Make the card into a picture post-card by drawing an illustration on the reverse side of the message.

Appendix:
Directory of Publishers

Harry N. Abrams, Inc.
100 Fifth Ave.
New York, NY 10011

Adama Publishers, Inc.
306 W. 38th St.
New York, NY 10018

Aladdin Books
Imprint of Macmillan
Publishing Co.
866 Third Ave.
New York, NY 10022

Atheneum
Imprint of Macmillan
Publishing Co.
866 Third Ave.
New York, NY 10022

Bantam Books, Inc.
666 Fifth Ave.
New York, NY 10103

Bradbury Press
Affil. of Macmillan, Inc.
866 Third Ave.
New York, NY 10022

Carolrhoda Books, Inc.
241 First Ave., N.
Minneapolis, MN 55401

Children's Press
5440 N. Cumberland Ave.
Chicago, IL 60656

Clarion
Imprint of Houghton Mifflin
Co.
1 Beacon St.
Boston, MA 02108

Cobblestone Publishing, Inc.
30 Grove St.
Peterborough, NH 03458

Coward-McCann Geoghegan
Imprint of Putnam Publishing
Group
200 Madison Ave.
New York, NY 10016

Creative Arts Book Co.
833 Bancroft Way
Berkeley, CA 94710

Thomas Y. Crowell
Imprint of Harper Collins
10 E. 53rd St.
New York, NY 10022

Crown Publishers, Inc.
225 Park Ave. S.
New York, NY 10003

Delacorte Press
1 Dag Hammarskjold Plaza
245 E. 47th Street
New York, NY 10017

Dial Books
Div. of E. P. Dutton
2 Park Ave.
New York, NY 10016

Dodd, Mead & Co.
71 Fifth Ave.
New York, NY 10003

Doubleday & Co.
666 Fifth Ave.
New York, NY 10103

E. P. Dutton
Div. of Penguin USA
2 Park Ave.
New York, NY 10016

Farrar, Straus and Giroux
19 Union Square West
New York, NY 1003

Four Winds Press
Imprint of Macmillan
Publishing Co.
866 Third Ave.
New York, NY 10022

Gallaudet University Press
800 Florida Ave., N.E.
Washington, DC 20002

Greenwillow Books
Division of William Morrow &
Co.
105 Madison Ave.
New York, NY 10016

Grossett & Dunlap
Imprint of Putnam Publishing
Group
200 Madison Ave.
New York, NY 10016

Hampstead Press
Imprint of Franklin Watts, Inc.
387 Park Ave., S.
New York, NY 10016

Harcourt Brace Jovanovich, Inc.
1250 Sixth Ave.
San Diego, CA 92101

Harper & Row
See Harper Collins

Harper Collins
10 E. 53rd St.
New York, NY 10022

Hastings House, Publishers
c/o Kampmann & Co.
226 W. 26th St.
New York, NY 10001

Henry Holt & Co.
115 W. 18th St.
New York, NY 10011

Holiday House, Inc.
18 E. 53rd St.
New York, NY 10022

Houghton Mifflin Co.
1 Beacon St.
Boston, MA 02108

Alfred A. Knopf, Inc.
Subs. of Random House, Inc.
201 E. 50th St.
New York, NY 10022

Lerner Publishing Co.
241 First Ave., N.
Minneapolis, MN 55401

J. B. Lippincott, Co.
Subs. of Harper Collins
E. Washington Sq.
Philadelphia, PA 19105

Little, Brown & Co.
34 Beacon St.
Boston, MA 02108

Lothrop, Lee & Shepard Books
Div. of William Morrow & Co.
105 Madison Ave.
New York, NY 10016

Macmillan Publishing Co., Inc.
866 Third Ave.
New York, NY 10022

William Morrow & Co., Inc.
105 Madison Ave.
New York, NY 10016

North-South Books
Dist. by Picture Book Studio
10 Central St.
Saxonville, MA 01701

Orchard Books
Div. of Franklin Watts, Inc.
387 Park Ave., S.
New York, NY 10016

Pantheon Books
Div. of Random House, Inc.
201 E. 50th St.
New York, NY 10022

Parents Magazine Press
685 Third Ave.
New York, NY 10017

Philomel Books
Imprint of Putnam Publishing
Group
200 Madison Ave.
New York, NY 10016

Prentice-Hall Press
Div. of Simon & Schuster
1 Gulf & Western Plaza
New York, NY 10023

G. P. Putnam's Sons
Imprint of Putnam Publishing
Group
200 Madison Ave.
New York, NY 10016

Raintree Publishers, Inc.
310 W. Wisconsin Ave.
Mezzanine Level
Milwaukee, WI 53203

Random House, Inc.
201 E. 50th St.
31st Floor
New York, NY 10022

Scholastic, Inc.
730 Broadway
New York, NY 10003

Charles Scribner's Sons
866 Third Ave.
New York, NY 10022

Simon & Schuster
1230 Ave. of the Americas
New York, NY 10020

Gareth Stevens, Inc.
7317 W. Green Tree Rd.
Milwaukee, WI 53223

Trails West Publishing
P. O. Box 8619
Santa Fe, NM 87504-8619

Viking Press
Subs. of Penguin USA
40 W. 23rd St.
New York, NY 10010

Walker Publishing Co.
720 Fifth Ave
New York, NY 10019

Frederick Warne & Co.
Div. of Viking Penguin, Inc.
40 W. 23rd St.
New York, NY 10010

Franklin Watts, Inc.
387 Park Ave., S.
New York, NY 10016

Western Publishing Co.
850 Third Ave.
New York, NY 10022

Westminster Press
100 Witherspoon St.
Louisville, KY 40202-1396

Albert Whitman
5745 W. Howard St.
Niles, IL 60648

H. W. Wilson
950 University Ave.
Bronx, NY 10452

Young Scott
Div. of Harper Collins
10 E. 53rd St.
New York, NY 10022

Index

by Linda Webster

MILDRED KNIGHT LAUGHLIN

Mildred Knight Laughlin is a professor in the School of Library and Information Studies at the University of Oklahoma. She, with Letty Watt, is the author of *Developing Learning Skills Through Children's Literature: An Idea Book for K-5 Classrooms and Libraries* (Oryx Press, 1986). With Claudia Swisher she wrote *Literature-Based Reading: Children's Books and Activities to Enrich the K-5 Curriculum* (Oryx Press, 1990). She has a B.A. in English from Fort Hays State University, Hays, Kansas; an M.A. in Education from Wichita State University, Wichita, Kansas; and an M.L.S. and a Ph.D in Education from the University of Oklahoma, Norman, Oklahoma.

PATRICIA KARDALEFF

Patricia Kardaleff holds a B.A. in speech/drama and a B.S. in elementary education from Cameron University in Lawton, Oklahoma. She received a Master's of Library and Information Studies from the University of Oklahoma in Norman, Oklahoma. She taught elementary social studies and reading for 10 years. She has been an elementary school library media specialist for the past five years.